BATTLE BETWEEN BEING
REWARDING YOURSELF.

A TRUCE.

a sedan that shows how smart you are.

The Nissan® Maxima® GXE.

It offers all the amenities you would expect to find in sedans costing twice as much: including a Digital Touch Keyless Entry System, air conditioning, power windows and door locks, AM/FM cassette with Dolby,® a sophisticated theft deterrent

system and optional equipment, such as a power sunroof, 4-way power adjustable driver's seat, compact disc player and seating surfaces appointed in leather.

Of course, what's under the hood is no less impressive. There you'll find a sequential, multi-point, fuel-injected 160 horsepower V6 that will ensure our interior doesn't make you too sedate.

If all of this is making the rational, right-side of your brain start to protest, consider that our '89 GXE has retained more of its original suggested price than either the '89 BMW 525i or the '89 Acura Legend Sedan.*

All of which suggests the only inner battle you'll have to face now is what color to pick.

NISSAN®

BUILT FOR THE
HUMAN RACE.

Forum

Vancouver

As a 12-year member of Vancouver's City Planning Commission, I have watched the transformation of this "Good Luck City" (April 1992) from a traditional post at the back door of a European-centered North America to one at the front door of an Asian-centered North America. The impact of immigrants has been profound. The wind-and-water art of *feng shui,* for example, has clashed head-on with old northern European sensibilities of land- and cityscaping.

The peoples of Asia are no more a monolith than the peoples of Europe ever were. Vancouver is learning just how diverse the Asian continent is, because Asia now is us.

ALAN HERBERT
Vancouver, British Columbia

No mention was made of the prolific Asian gang problem or of the criminals from Hong Kong triads, mainland China, and Vietnam who enter under Canada's refugee program and set up shop. The price of land is being driven up by demand from the Pacific Rim, and there is a feeling that our culture is being smothered. Enormous numbers of Vancouverites are fed up.

EDWARD G. RAYNER
North Vancouver, British Columbia

I was upset by the photographs of captured beluga whales. Belugas are very intelligent mammals with complex social behavior. To satisfy the market for live marine mammals, they are hunted down and traumatized by the chase. Those that survive end up in watery prisons with strangers. An aquarium, no matter how large, does not compare to open water. Your cover will stimulate the demand for these creatures.

YVONNE MICHEL
Yonges Island, South Carolina

Spain

I would recommend that uninformed tourists read the bright and wise article by Bill Bryson. It will give them essential clues to understanding our changing Spain and its cultural diversity. Unfortunately, the pictures focus again on well-known Andalusian subjects such as polka-dot dresses, flamenco, and bullfighting.

ANNA BUXADERAS
Barcelona, Spain

Author Bryson says that "thinking of tomorrow is an alien concept in Spain." Young Spanish scientists and researchers have never been so convinced of that till now, when the government has sacrificed science to save money. Does anyone know how much the Olympic Games, Expo '92, and cultural events in Madrid will cost Spain's development? I am sure that the world now understands why Spain is (and will be) a country of bullfighters, *nazarenos,* and nationalists and not one of scientists and investigators.

JERÓNIMO J. GÓMEZ
Madrid, Spain

The influence of the thousand years of Jewish participation in Spain was omitted. The Jews contributed greatly to the economy, arts, philosophy, and sciences of that country until their expulsion in 1492 by Ferdinand and Isabella.

ELAINE L. PRAG
Chicago, Illinois

The delicate issue of Basque terrorism is treated with the opinions of a journalist from a newspaper that supports the terrorists and a politician who claims the Basque country is a police state. Spain is a democracy. Even the politician Josu Cerrato can speak freely, and human rights are respected. The problems of the Basque region are very complex; car bombs, assassinations, and terror will not solve them. More than 80 percent of the voters in recent elections in the region voted for political parties that oppose terrorism.

FERNANDO DOÑATE
Kansas City, Missouri

In the March 15 elections to the Catalan Parliament, 55 percent of the people who voted cast their ballots for Catalan parties and made an openly separatist party the third largest in Catalonia. The day may not be far away when Catalonia regains its independence in the newly shaped Europe.

MARSAL GAVALDÀ
Barcelona, Spain

The major party in Catalonia remains staunchly opposed to separatism.

Lion Survey

I was most interested to read your story on the Ngorongoro Crater lions and the problem of inbreeding. For some years now scientists have been distributing animal sperm to many countries using cold storage or animal hosts. Could this method of breeding be applied to the Ngorongoro lions? There are many lions in captivity that could be used as donors to encourage healthy propagation of the gene pool in a controlled environment such as that the crater offers.

MAY SHEPPARD
Wellington, New Zealand

If the situation in the crater becomes critical, artificial insemination or relocation may be considered.

Sometimes the finest serve comes after the game.

After a close round of tennis, enjoy a round of caffeine free diet Coke® *Just for the taste*

Caffeine Free **diet Coke**

Trademarks ®

Official Serve of the U.S. Open and Wimbledon.

While these methods have worked with captive animals, they pose enormous logistical problems in the wild.

Simpson Outback

It seems to me, a resident of an outer suburb of Adelaide, that the majority of your articles dealing with Australia deal with the uninhabited outback. Three-fifths of the 17 million people in Australia live in the five largest cities, and many of the rest live in smaller population centers. The majority of us are less likely to visit the outback in a year than an American, British, or Japanese tourist. The true picture of a modern Australian is that of a city dweller.

DUNCAN RICHER
Salisbury Heights, South Australia

This beautifully done article brought back memories. I was involved in oil exploration in the Simpson Desert in the mid-1960s. The temperature in the dining tent was sometimes 128°F. The flies swarmed all over you, getting into your ears, eyes, mouth, and nose. We looked forward to the wind coming up so we could get a respite from the flies. We went to Alice Springs for supplies, and I'll always remember the natural friendliness of the Australian people.

BOYD HUDSON
Bathurst, New Brunswick

Blackwater Country

As a former resident of this Florida-Georgia borderland, I enjoyed the insight that Richard Conniff's article offered. The photographs, however, miss the distinctive low-ground, water-level look of the place. Those who live there don't see it from airplanes or in wide-angle close-ups. Where are the views of small towns and blackwater rivers we love?

LAWRENCE HETRICK
Duluth, Georgia

Last spring four of us had the time of our lives on Cumberland Island National Seashore. The only damper was the potent odor of Gilman's paper mill; it was an awakening to the reality of modern paper conveniences. The people of southeastern Georgia will have to settle on a happy medium. From the paper company come jobs, revenue, and pollution. From Cumberland Island and Okefenokee comes the beauty of preservation.

ERIK R. LINDEN
Washington, D. C.

Earth Almanac

The implication that acid rain and air pollutants have caused the "loss of millions of maples native to Canada and the eastern United States" is wrong. Recent studies have demonstrated that maples in general, and sugar maple specifically, are increasing in growth and productivity across their entire range. Severe defoliations by insect pests and drought along with severe winter freezes have all been demonstrated as significant and well-described causes of decline at specific sites, but acid rain should no longer be considered as having a role.

JOHN M. SKELLY
Pennsylvania State University
University Park, Pennsylvania

Geographica

I was very pleased that our recent discovery of the dispersers of *Rafflesia* seeds was featured in the April issue. However, the finding was not my own but a collaborative effort with two Malaysian coworkers, Alim Biun and Jamili Nais, the latter in fact being the man in the photograph. All of us contributed equally to the effort.

LOUISE H. EMMONS
National Museum of Natural History
Washington, D. C.

Forum

In Mr. Nisbet's letter in April, the listing of people united under Field Marshal Alexander in Italy ought to be rectified: Not "Palestinians (including Jews)" but almost exclusively Jews. Thirty thousand Jewish soldiers from Palestine—volunteers all—served in World War II, including 5,000 in the Jewish Infantry Brigade. I am a former officer with Italy frontline service in the said Jewish Brigade.

DANIEL OR
Tel Aviv, Israel

Alcohol

In the feature on alcohol (February 1992), the writer acknowledges, briefly, that the vast majority of people drink harmlessly and sensibly. Yet the great emphasis of the feature was on the small, sad minority who misuse. Since the beginning of history most of mankind has found enjoyment and sociability in alcoholic beverages. An increasing body of independent medical research from the U. S., New Zealand, Japan, and elsewhere identifies moderate consumption as an aid to healthy living, a point only marginally noted. Worldwide, the industry devotes significant resources to encourage moderate, sensible enjoyment of alcohol and help combat misuse by a minority of users. These unfortunate people are the exception; they are not the large majority of drinkers. This is the important perspective not to be overlooked.

A. J. TENNANT
Chairman, Guinness PLC
London, England

Letters should be addressed to FORUM, *National Geographic Magazine, Box 37448, Washington, D. C. 20013, and should include sender's address and telephone number. Not all letters can be used. Those that are will often be edited and excerpted.*

Ever wo
it's called a t

In case you were wondering, this is the Honda Gold Wing motorcycle. Technically speaking, what you'd call a luxury touring bike. Our engineers designed it especially for adventurous motorcycling enthusiasts who like to cover great distances at a time.

Yet, some of the longest trips it ever makes are from our shipping docks at the Honda motorcycle plant in Marysville, Ohio.

You see, that's the only place in the world where we make them. And have for ten years. In fact, Honda was among the first Japanese companies to ever manufacture motorcycles in America. That early

success helped pave the way for our automotive, power equipment and engine plants throughout the United States. A total capital investment from Honda of more than $1.7 billion to date.

nder why ouring bike?

Today, the Marysville facility is one of the most technically advanced and efficient factories of its kind. Which might explain why Honda sells more motorcycles than any other company in America. Not to mention the world.

As with any Honda product, our associates make sure each piece and part,

no matter how small, measures up to Honda standards. And that's no easy task by anyone's standards.

From our appearance inspections that check the things you can see, to dynamometer tests that check the things you can't, nothing is ever overlooked. Nothing.

It's then, and only then, that a Honda Gold Wing touring bike is stamped for approval and ready to be shipped. Some to those as close as Canada, and others as far away as New Zealand. All who turn to America for some of the world's best-built motorcycles. Wonders will never cease.

HONDA

The Orphans
Help Us, Help Them

This orphaned elephant is well cared for in the United States. Not all orphaned African elephants survive without the protection of their mother, if they survive at all.

Orphaned Elephant

The innocent victims that remain after entire families have been killed for their ivory are the orphaned infant and young elephants. Most are severely traumatized having witnessed this loss. Due to their young age, they can not care for themselves. Because elephants have lifespans and developmental stages similar to humans, the fortunate ones that are rescued will require care for the next 15 years, or until they can survive on their own.

Help us give them the chance for life they deserve.

The Dragonette Society for the Preservation of Endangered Animals, Inc., is a non-profit organization dedicated to preserving threatened or endangered species. The funds we raise are advanced to the direct needs of these animals.

If you would like to help by sending greatly needed contributions or would like information on this Orphaned Elephant poster, please write to:

THE DRAGONETTE SOCIETY
FOR THE PRESERVATION OF ENDANGERED ANIMALS, INC.
P.O. Box 669606, Marietta, GA 30066

CONTRIBUTIONS ARE TAX-DEDUCTIBLE TO THE FULL EXTENT OF THE LAW.

...get very far. A girl with no direction in her life doesn't...

At Girls Incorporated, we have a very simple mission: to help young women chart their own direction for the future. It's one we've successfully followed for almost 50 years under the name of Girls Clubs of America.

Our name changed because, quite frankly, growing up has. Our new name not only better reflects the times, but also what we're doing. Working to give every girl the power and confidence to go pl~ Instead of in circles.

30 East 33rd Street New Yor

A stunning scientific journal from National Geographic!

RESEARCH & EXPLORATION

Examine this colorful, visually appealing journal from National Geographic and learn about new discoveries in scientific disciplines ranging from anthropology to zoology. *Research & Exploration*'s readable format makes it appropriate for scientists, educators, and informed readers worldwide.

Each issue includes commentary, opinions, and reviews of current books. Only $40 for four quarterly issues. To order, call toll free **1-800-638-4077**, Monday-Friday, 8 a.m. to 4 p.m. ET. Or write:

NATIONAL GEOGRAPHIC SOCIETY
Box 1111, Washington, D.C. 20013-9990

Zoos have had difficulty breeding pandas. Even China's Wolong Preserve, a protected habitat in the panda's natural range, has had limited success in its captive breeding program.

Adapting To Change Isn't Easy. Maybe That's Why So Many Insurance Companies Don't Even Try.

Adapting to change is a fact of life. Even for an insurance company. Because today, insurance can't protect you unless it can change.

For that reason, Mutual of Omaha offers an individually tailored approach to insurance that allows it to evolve and change as your needs do, throughout your life.

Sound too good to be true? Well, it's not business as usual. But it is what you'd expect from a company with a history of concern for our changing world.

Look into it. Because if your insurance company hasn't changed in years, maybe it's time to change your insurance company.

MutualᵒᶠOmaha Companies

Protecting You In Ways No One Ever Thought Of Before.

Geographica

MANOOCHER

A Super(nova) Mystery: Where's the Pulsar?

"A star blowing up is not an orderly process," says Roger A. Chevalier, a University of Virginia astronomer.

Five years after the detection of supernova 1987A (GEOGRAPHIC, May 1988), scientists are elated that observations have validated many of their theories of how a star becomes a supernova. But they are puzzled by several surprises, including a big one: Where is the rotating neutron star, or pulsar, that theory says the explosion should have created?

Astronomers have confirmed that the star Sanduleak -69°202 in the Large Magellanic Cloud—the galaxy nearest our own—was about 170,000 light-years from earth when its core collapsed and the star exploded. They saw the gases it had "exhaled" well before the explosion, detected particles called neutrinos the collapsing star sent hurtling into the cosmos, and picked up radio emissions indicating that the gases flooding out of the supernova are starting to collide with other gases in the "neighborhood." They even photographed twin light echoes as the flash of radiation from the dying star passed through two sheets of dust (below).

Still, says Robert P. Kirshner of Harvard, "the big surprise is what didn't happen: No one has seen the pulsar yet."

Colossal Statue Hints at Major Ramses Temple

Yahya al-Masri, the director of antiquities in Egypt's Sohag region, hoped he would see something historically interesting when workers began to dig the foundation for a post office in the town of Akhmim on the east bank of the River Nile. After all, crews there working under his supervision in 1981 had found part of a temple containing fractured statues of Ramses II and one of his wives.

Yet even Masri was startled late last year by what the workers discovered: a huge hieroglyph-covered limestone statue of a seated Ramses, nearly 50 feet long, whose severed head turned up a few feet away. Another statue found nearby in several pieces may be of an ancient queen.

The discoveries confirm tales of ancient travelers that the little-studied, little-known Sohag area— 300 miles south of Cairo—held a major temple of Ramses the Great, the pharaoh who ruled Egypt for more than 60 years in the 13th century B.C. (NATIONAL GEOGRAPHIC, April 1991). Work at the site, on a hill in the middle of Akhmim, has been halted while Masri and his team determine how to proceed without causing an adjacent cemetery to collapse.

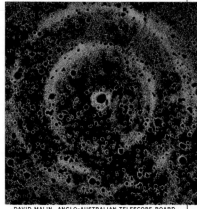

DAVID MALIN, ANGLO-AUSTRALIAN TELESCOPE BOARD

Bob Ottenbacher: Ford Employee

"I build the engine that broke the tradition."

Traditionally, overhead cam V-8 engines have been found only in expensive imported cars. Ford Motor Company changed all that. Our 4.6 liter overhead cam V-8 captures the brilliant performance and the exhilarating power that has long been out of reach, and puts it under the hood of a Ford, Lincoln or Mercury.

Ford • Lincoln • Mercury • Ford Trucks

QUALITY IS JOB 1.[SM] IT'S WORKING.

Buckle up–Together we can save lives.

Always insist on genuine Ford Motor Company collision repair parts.

If you would like a large, easy-to-read version of the information below, call 1-800-3M-ANSWERS (1-800-362-6793).

MINITRAN™
(nitroglycerin)
TRANSDERMAL DELIVERY SYSTEM

BRIEF SUMMARY

INDICATIONS AND USAGE

This drug product has been conditionally approved by the FDA for the prevention of angina pectoris due to coronary artery disease. Tolerance to the anti-anginal effects of nitrates (measured by exercise stress testing) has been shown to be a major factor limiting efficacy when transdermal nitrates are used continuously for longer than 12 hours each day. The development of tolerance can be altered (prevented or attenuated) by use of a noncontinuous (intermittent) dosing schedule with a nitrate-free interval of 10–12 hours.

Controlled clinical trial data suggest that the intermittent use of nitrates is associated with decreased exercise tolerance, in comparison to placebo, during the last part of the nitrate-free interval; the clinical relevance of this observation is unknown, but the possibility of increased frequency or severity of angina during the nitrate-free interval should be considered. Further investigations of the tolerance phenomenon and best regimen are ongoing. A final evaluation of the effectiveness of the product will be announced by the FDA.

CONTRAINDICATIONS: Allergic reactions to organic nitrates are extremely rare, but they do occur. Nitroglycerin is contraindicated in patients who are allergic to it. Allergy to the adhesives used in nitroglycerin patches has also been reported, and it similarly constitutes a contraindication to the use of this product. **WARNINGS:** The benefits of transdermal nitroglycerin in patients with acute myocardial infarction or congestive heart failure have not been established. If one elects to use nitroglycerin in these conditions, careful clinical or hemodynamic monitoring must be used to avoid the hazards of hypotension and tachycardia. A cardiovertor/defibrillator should not be discharged through a paddle electrode that overlies a MINITRAN patch. The arcing that may be seen in this situation is harmless in itself, but it may be associated with local current concentration that can cause damage to the paddles and burns to the patient. **PRECAUTIONS:** General: Severe hypotension, particularly with upright posture, may occur with even small doses of nitroglycerin. This drug should therefore be used with caution in patients who may be volume depleted or who, for whatever reason, are already hypotensive. Hypotension induced by nitroglycerin may be accompanied by paradoxical bradycardia and increased angina pectoris. Nitrate therapy may aggravate the angina caused by hypertrophic cardiomyopathy. As tolerance to other forms of nitroglycerin develops, the effect of sublingual nitroglycerin on exercise tolerance, although still observable, is somewhat blunted. In industrial workers who have had long-term exposure to unknown (presumably high) doses of organic nitrates, tolerance clearly occurs. Chest pain, acute myocardial infarction, and even sudden death have occurred during temporary withdrawal of nitrates from these workers, demonstrating the existence of true physical dependence. Several clinical trials in patients with angina pectoris have evaluated nitroglycerin regimens which incorporated a 10–12 hour nitrate-free interval. In some of these trials, an increase in the frequency of anginal attacks during the nitrate-free interval was observed in a small number of patients. In one trial, patients demonstrated decreased exercise tolerance at the end of the nitrate-free interval. Hemodynamic rebound has been observed only rarely; on the other hand, few studies were so designed that rebound, if it had occurred, would have been detected. The importance of these observations to the routine, clinical use of transdermal nitroglycerin is unknown. **Information for Patients:** Daily headaches sometimes accompany treatment with nitroglycerin. In patients who get these headaches, the headache may be a marker of the activity of the drug. Patients should resist the temptation to avoid headaches by altering the schedule of their treatment with nitroglycerin, since loss of headache may be associated with simultaneous loss of anti-anginal efficacy. Treatment with nitroglycerin may be associated with lightheadedness on standing, especially just after rising from a recumbent or seated position. This effect may be more frequent in patients who have also consumed alcohol. After normal use, there is enough residual nitroglycerin in discarded patches that they are a potential hazard to children and pets. A patient leaflet is supplied with the systems. **Drug Interactions:** The vasodilating effects of nitroglycerin may be additive with those of other vasodilators. Alcohol, in particular, has been found to exhibit additive effects of this variety. **Carcinogenesis, Mutagenesis, and Impairment of Fertility:** No long-term animal studies have examined the carcinogenic or mutagenic potential of nitroglycerin. Nitroglycerin's effect upon reproductive capacity is similarly unknown. **Pregnancy Category C:** Animal reproduction studies have not been conducted on nitroglycerin. It is also not known whether nitroglycerin can cause fetal harm when administered to a pregnant woman or whether it can affect reproductive capacity. Nitroglycerin should be given to a pregnant woman only if clearly needed. **Nursing Mothers:** It is not known whether nitroglycerin is excreted in human milk. Because many drugs are excreted in human milk, caution should be exercised when nitroglycerin is administered to a nursing woman. **Pediatric Use:** Safety and effectiveness in children have not been established. **ADVERSE REACTIONS:** Adverse reactions to nitroglycerin are generally dose-related, and almost all of these reactions are the result of nitroglycerin's activity as a vasodilator. Headache, which may be severe, is the most commonly reported side effect. Headache may be recurrent with each daily dose, especially at higher doses. Transient episodes of lightheadedness, occasionally related to blood pressure changes, may also occur. Hypotension occurs infrequently, but in some patients it may be severe enough to warrant discontinuation of therapy. Syncope, crescendo angina, and rebound hypertension have been reported but are uncommon. Extremely rarely, ordinary doses of organic nitrates have caused methemoglobinemia in normal-seeming patients. Methemoglobinemia is so infrequent at these doses that further discussion of its diagnosis and treatment is deferred (see **Overdosage**). Application-site irritation may occur but is rarely severe. In two placebo-controlled trials of intermittent therapy with nitroglycerin patches at 0.2 to 0.8 mg/hr, the most frequent adverse reactions among 307 subjects were as follows:

	placebo	patch		placebo	patch
headache	18%	63%	hypotension and/or syncope	0%	4%
lightheadedness	4%	6%	increased angina	2%	2%

OVERDOSAGE: Hemodynamic Effects: The ill effects of nitroglycerin overdose are generally the results of nitroglycerin's capacity to induce vasodilatation, venous pooling, reduced cardiac output, and hypotension. These hemodynamic changes may have protean manifestations, including increased intracranial pressure, with any or all of persistent throbbing headache, confusion, and moderate fever; vertigo; palpitations; visual disturbances; nausea and vomiting (possibly with colic and even bloody diarrhea); syncope (especially in the upright posture); air hunger and dyspnea, later followed by reduced ventilatory effort; diaphoresis, with the skin either flushed or cold and clammy; heart block and bradycardia; paralysis; coma; seizures; and death. Laboratory determinations of serum levels of nitroglycerin and its metabolites are not widely available, and such determinations have, in any event, no established role in the management of nitroglycerin overdose. No data are available to suggest physiological maneuvers (e.g., maneuvers to change the pH of the urine) that might accelerate elimination of nitroglycerin and its active metabolites. Similarly, it is not known which – if any – of these substances can usefully be removed from the body by hemodialysis. No specific antagonist to the vasodilator effects of nitroglycerin is known, and no intervention has been subject to controlled study as a therapy of nitroglycerin overdose. Because the hypotension associated with nitroglycerin overdose is the result of venodilatation and arterial hypovolemia, prudent therapy in this situation should be directed toward increase in central fluid volume. Passive elevation of the patient's legs may be sufficient, but intravenous infusion of normal saline or similar fluid may also be necessary. The use of epinephrine or other arterial vasoconstrictors in this setting is likely to do more harm than good. In patients with renal disease or congestive heart failure, therapy resulting in central volume expansion is not without hazard. Treatment of nitroglycerin overdose in these patients may be subtle and difficult, and invasive monitoring may be required. **Methemoglobinemia:** Nitrate ions liberated during metabolism of nitroglycerin can oxidize hemoglobin into methemoglobin. Even in patients totally without cytochrome b_5 reductase activity, however, and even assuming that nitrate moieties of nitroglycerin are quantitatively applied to oxidation of hemoglobin, about 1 mg/kg of nitroglycerin should be required before any of these patients manifests clinically significant ($\geq$10%) methemoglobinemia. In patients with normal reductase function, significant production of methemoglobin should require even larger doses of nitroglycerin. In one study in which 36 patients received 2–4 weeks of continuous nitroglycerin therapy at 3.1 to 4.4 mg/hr, the average methemoglobin level measured was 0.2%; this was comparable to that observed in parallel patients who received placebo. Notwithstanding these observations, there are case reports of significant methemoglobinemia in association with moderate overdoses of organic nitrates. None of the affected patients had been thought to be unusually susceptible. Methemoglobin levels are available from most clinical laboratories. The diagnosis should be suspected in patients who exhibit signs of impaired oxygen delivery despite adequate cardiac output and adequate arterial pO_2. Classically, methemoglobinemic blood is described as chocolate brown, without color change on exposure to air. When methemoglobinemia is diagnosed, the treatment of choice is methylene blue, 1–2 mg/kg intravenously. **DOSAGE AND ADMINISTRATION:** The suggested starting dose is between 0.2 mg/hr* and 0.4 mg/hr*. Doses between 0.4 mg/hr* and 0.8 mg/hr* have shown continued effectiveness for 10–12 hours daily for at least one month (the longest period studied) of intermittent administration. Although the minimum nitrate-free interval has not been defined, data show that a nitrate-free interval of 10–12 hours is sufficient (see **Clinical Pharmacology**). Thus, an appropriate dosing schedule for nitroglycerin patches would include a daily patch-on period of 12–14 hours and a daily patch-off period of 10–12 hours. Although some well-controlled clinical trials using exercise tolerance testing have shown maintenance of effectiveness when patches are worn continuously, the large majority of such controlled trials have shown the development of tolerance (i.e., complete loss of effect) within the first 24 hours after therapy was initiated. Dose adjustment, even to levels much higher than generally used, did not restore efficacy. **STORAGE CONDITIONS:** Store at controlled room temperature 15°–30°C (59°–86°F). Extremes of temperature and/or humidity should be avoided. **CAUTION:** Federal law prohibits dispensing without prescription.

*Release rates were formerly described in terms of drug delivered per 24 hours. In these terms, the supplied MINITRAN systems would be rated at 2.5 mg/ 24 hours (0.1 mg/hr), 5 mg/24 hours (0.2 mg/hr), 10 mg/24 hours (0.4 mg/hr), and 15 mg/24 hours (0.6 mg/hr).

3M Pharmaceuticals
Northridge, CA 91324

NTR-6BS   JUNE 1991

REFERENCES: 1. Hougham AJ, Hawkinson RW, Crowley JK, et al. *Clin Ther.* 1989;11(1):15–31. **2.** Pharmaceutical Data Services; Scottsdale, AZ: Jan 1992. Retail pricing may vary from community to community and may affect cost savings to the patient. Transderm-Nitro is a registered trademark of Ciba Pharmaceutical Co; Nitro-Dur, of Key Pharmaceuticals, Inc.
Minitran is not available in Canada and Mexico.
© 3M Pharmaceuticals — 1992   2300-17263MP-NG

3M Pharmaceuticals
3M Health Care
St. Paul, Minnesota 55144-1000

Can you tell who's wearing the nitroglycerin patch?

The truth is both are. The twin on the right is wearing Transderm-Nitro®. The twin on the left is wearing Minitran — the smallest, thinnest, most transparent nitroglycerin patch.

When asked about such product features as size, transparency and adhesion, patch wearers preferred Minitran more than 2 to 1 over Transderm-Nitro and Nitro-Dur®.[1] There's one more thing to like — Minitran should cost less than your current brand.[2]

Want to know more about Minitran? Ask your doctor or pharmacist, or call 1-800-3M-ANSWERS (1-800-362-6793).

All transdermal nitroglycerin products are being marketed pending final evaluation of effectiveness by the FDA.

Please see adjacent page for summary of prescribing information.

Innovation working for you ™

MINITRAN™
(nitroglycerin)
TRANSDERMAL DELIVERY SYSTEM
0.1 MG/HR, 0.2 MG/HR, 0.4 MG/HR, 0.6 MG/HR
The small wonder.

3M Pharmaceuticals
3M Health Care
St. Paul, Minnesota 55144-1000

3M

Geographica

Shrunken-Head Buyers Beware!

Here's a warning for souvenir hunters traveling in Ecuador: That shrunken head for sale is probably not the head of a slain enemy warrior like those traditionally crafted by the forest-dwelling Shuar people, also known as the Jívaro. Instead it could be made of animal skin—or it could be the head of a human who died naturally.

Robert W. Mann, a physical anthropologist, studied several shrunken heads in the Smithsonian Institution's collection and four others purchased by tourists in South America since 1986. All purportedly were Jívaro trophy heads. But Mann found—largely by examining the facial features and hair attached to each head—that only those obtained in the late 19th or early 20th century were genuine.

True Jívaro trophy heads, one-fourth to one-eighth normal size, have severely distorted faces (top, at left); the recently purchased ones do not, probably because Shuar elders have not passed down traditional head-shrinking customs, Mann says.

The Ecuadorian government long has banned traffic in shrunken heads, as an October 1921 GEO-GRAPHIC article about the Jívaro noted. But, says Mann, "as long as demand exists, it will be met one way or another."

Is This the Adam or Eve of All Modern Insects?

It bears an unwieldy name—euthycarcinoid, from the Greek for "straight crab"—and looks unwieldy as well, with 16 segments, 11 of which carry a pair of legs each. A Western Australian Museum

VICTOR R. BOSWELL, JR., NGS

paleontologist, Ken McNamara, thinks all insects descended from creatures like the five-inch-long, 420-million-year-old fossil he found in Australia's Murchison gorge.

Before McNamara's find, the earliest euthycarcinoid had been dated at 310 million years, 65 million years later than the oldest known insect. The new discovery means that euthycarcinoids predated insects, and McNamara believes

ROGER GARWOOD

their 11 pairs of legs evolved into the three pairs typical of insects.

McNamara admits the jury is still out. Like insects—and unlike the centipede, the other prime candidate for the role of insect ancestor—euthycarcinoid bodies contained a separate thorax and abdomen. But centipede heads more closely resemble insect heads.

Euthycarcinoids lived in fresh water but probably ventured onto land, McNamara suggests. As insects evolved, they became smaller. "In a world dominated by predators, one good way to survive would have been by being small," he says. "This small size also may have made it easier to adapt to living permanently out of water."

Using DNA to Identify Future Unknown Soldiers

Maj. Victor Weedn doesn't use the term "DNA dog tag." Still, he understands why "everybody but me" is using it to describe the DNA repository he is establishing at the Armed Forces Institute of Pathology in Washington, D. C.

Weedn, chief of the institute's DNA identification laboratory, says the repository will serve the same purpose as a set of dog tags: to aid in identifying a dead body, whether a fatality of war or of a disaster such as a plane crash.

"Dog tags are not considered positive proof of identification," he says. "DNA profiling can be, because everyone's DNA is unique" (GEOGRAPHIC, May 1992).

To set up the repository, the armed forces will take blood samples and oral swabs from new recruits; eventually all members of the armed forces will provide them. If the body of a military person cannot be identified through fingerprints or dental records, DNA from its tissues will be compared with DNA in the repository.

DNA samples will remain private, Weedn says. They will be treated like other medical specimens, kept under strict security and made available only under court order.

—BORIS WEINTRAUB

LeSabre for 1992.
Ladies and gentlemen,
start your comparisons.

	'92 Buick LeSabre Limited	'92 Toyota Cressida Sedan
Engine	3.8-litre V6	3.0-litre Inline 6
Drivetrain	Front Drive	Rear Drive
Passenger Room	109.2 cu ft	89.0 cu ft
Trunk Room	17.0 cu ft	12.5 cu ft
Anti-Lock Brakes	Standard	Optional
Driver Air Bag	Standard	Not Available
M.S.R.P.*	**$21,100**	**$25,558**

All new, all Buick

When you compare the 1992 LeSabre Limited to its import competition, one thing stands out — the value built into this new Buick.

In key areas — from engine capacity to trunk capacity, from passenger room to a driver air bag — Buick LeSabre gives you more.

Yet LeSabre asks less of you in return. Thousands of dollars less.

So go ahead and start your comparisons. We're confident you'll end up behind the wheel of a new Buick LeSabre.

For more information on LeSabre quality and value, call 1-800-531-1115, or visit your Buick dealer and take a test drive today.

BUICK
The New Symbol For Quality
In America.

Toyota Cressida

Buick LeSabre

WHEN WE INVENTED 8MM, WE NEVER REALIZED HOW MANY LIVES WE'D BE SAVING.

Since you can't re-invent precious moments, we invented the ideal way to save them.

After conceiving the tiny 8mm video cassette and camcorder back in 1975, Sony Recording Media has produced tens of millions of cherished memories. And touched thousands of lives with a very special legacy.

So look into this year's new family of startlingly clear 8mm video cassettes and find the perfect fit for your family.

We invented the tape. Now you go invent the moments.

SONY

SONY RECORDING MEDIA

The World's Toughest 4x4 Is The Only One With A Soft Spot.

The New Jeep® Grand Cherokee Limited

There's Only One Jeep®...
Advantage: Chrysler

 Chrysler's Owner's Choice Protection Plan includes: 7-year/70,000-mile powertrain protection or 3-year/36,000-mile bumper-to-bumper warranty. Your choice. And with no deductible. See limited warranties, restrictions, and details at dealer. Excludes normal maintenance, adjustments, and wear items. For further information about Jeep Grand Cherokee, call 1-800-JEEP-EAGLE. Jeep is a registered trademark of Chrysler Corporation. Buckle up for safety.

OFFICIAL SPONSOR OF THE 1992 **U S A**
U.S. OLYMPIC TEAM 36 USC 380

NATIONAL GEOGRAPHIC

AUGUST 1992

COVER: His village destroyed in 1988, this Iraqi Kurd now lives on a guerrilla base with countrymen fighting Saddam Hussein. Photograph by Ed Kashi.
♻ Cover printed on recycled-content paper.

FOR MEMBERSHIP INFORMATION CALL 1-800-638-4077

Main-Danube Canal

LINKING EUROPE'S WATERWAYS

Calm highway of water, a new German ship canal crosses the European watershed south of Nürnberg, linking the Main, a tributary of the Rhine River, to the Danube. After the long-awaited opening in September, the route will connect hundreds of inland ports from the North Sea to the Black Sea.

By BILL BRYSON
Photographs by GERD LUDWIG

Sweeping across rural Bavaria, the broad canal horseshoes through the lower Altmühl Valley—some say, ruining it. Designed for minimum

environmental impact, this stretch incorporates a large lake for swimming and artificial ponds for wildlife along landscaped banks.

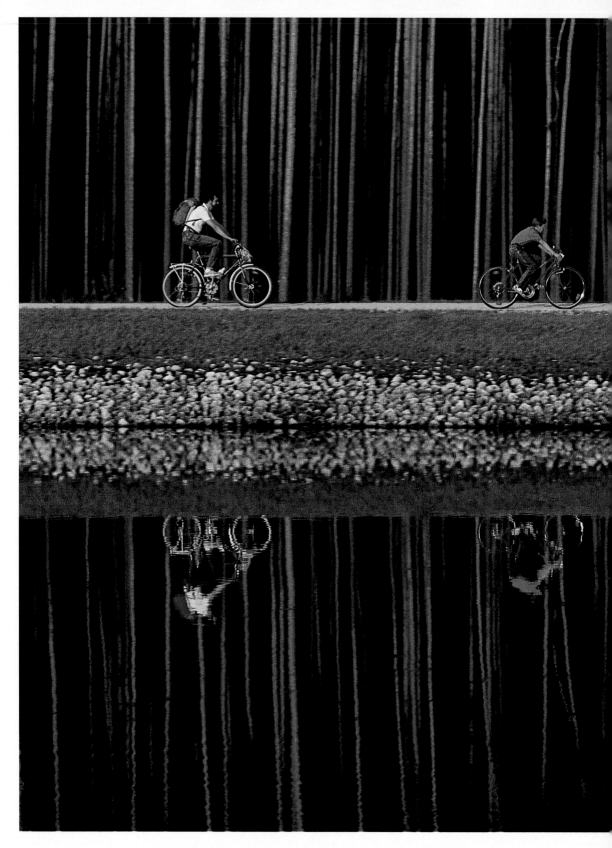

Quiet flows the canal through a dense pine forest outside Nürnberg.
Paths were built along both sides of the 106-mile canal to give access

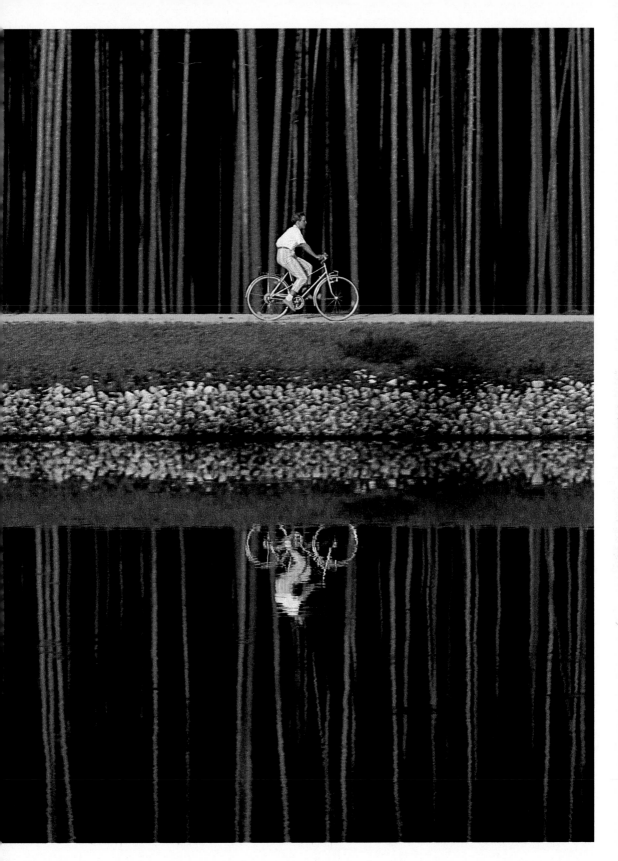

for repairs and emergencies and to open new routes through country scenery for cyclists and hikers.

ON THE EDGE of a sunny field in an almost forgotten corner of Bavaria there stands an incongruous sight: a stone monument built around an old-fashioned, long-handled pump from which water flows in two directions—to the left and to the right. Set on Europe's continental divide, it is there to make a point. Water flowing to the right will find its way to the Main River and onward to the Rhine and the North Sea, 600 winding miles to the north. Water draining to the left will run in a contrary direction, heading south and east for the Danube and on to the Black Sea, 1,350 miles distant.

The pump was erected by the Bavarian state government as a diversion for passers-by, but for well over a thousand years people have known that this is, geographically speaking, an almost magical spot: a place where two great river systems come tantalizingly close to touching.

A canal running only three miles between the Rivers Altmühl and Schwäbische Rezat would connect the two. For the sake of 5,500 yards of digging, you would get access to 2,000 miles of navigable waterway. In A.D. 793, Emperor Charlemagne decided the mathematics were too tempting to ignore. He set an army of men to work digging an eight-foot-deep trench just outside the present-day village of Graben (the name means "trench" in German).

Today, his project, the Fossa Carolina, can still be seen, just a hundred yards or so from the watershed pump. It inhabits a wild and oddly melancholy stretch of woodland, a curving pool of still, green water cut off from the world by a dense overhang of leaves and a tangle of thorny undergrowth. For all its

forlornness, it still looks remarkably navigable, but this is an illusion.

The Fossa Carolina was never deep enough to accommodate the difference in elevation between the two small rivers it was intended to connect. Charlemagne's men dug and dug, but as the trench repeatedly filled with water under heavy rains, the banks turned into an unstable ooze. Frustrated, and with more pressing problems beckoning from elsewhere within his empire, Charlemagne abandoned the project after just two months.

Now, 1,199 years later, Charlemagne's dream is about to be realized on a scale beyond his wildest imaginings. The Main-Danube Canal, nearing completion 30 miles east of Graben, will link not only the Rhine and Danube river systems but also (thanks to other canals already in existence) much of the European waterway network. In

September, for the first time, a heavy barge will be able to travel from, say, Strasbourg to Bucharest without ever turning to the sea. The question is whether anyone much will want to.

"A canal is used not because it is there, but because there is a need for it," says Eugen Wirth, a professor of physical geography at the University of Erlangen-Nürnberg and one of many vocal critics of the project. "And the need for this canal has never been demonstrated."

Whether the Main-Danube Canal proves to be a prescient and lucrative conduit to the newly emerging markets of Eastern Europe, as its builders hope, or a costly white elephant, as many others believe, it is certainly an impressive engineering achievement.

Running for 106 miles between Bamberg, where the Regnitz feeds into the Main River, and Kelheim, on the Danube, and climbing and dropping a total of 800 feet as it crosses the Fränkische Alb, it winds through some of the most challenging, scenic, and environmentally sensitive landscape in Germany. It is this last factor that lies behind a long and often passionate ground swell of opposition.

"It is the biggest *Sauerei* of the century," Eduard Steichele, director of tourism for the picturesque cathedral town of Eichstätt, told me, employing a piece of porcine Bavarian slang that is as emphatic as it is inelegant. "Even if the canal is an economic success, and that is by no means certain, the cost in terms of destruction to the Altmühl Valley is unforgivable."

This valley, with Eichstätt at its heart, is one of the most beautiful and environmentally fragile in Bavaria. Etched by the small and winding Altmühl River, it is lined with small farms and drowsing villages, punctuated with the spires of old churches, and hemmed in by jagged hills cloaked with beech and pine. Towering above the valley floor are outcrops of limestone where storybook castles perch, looking at once wildly romantic and impossibly inaccessible.

An object lesson in progress, the 1845 canal built by King Ludwig I of Bavaria lost business after railroads came. The question now: Can the new canal—a few wingbeats from this relic-turned-nature-preserve at Prunn—compete with efficient but more costly railway systems?

Flanked by forbidding hills and dense forests, it is an area where time moves at a different pace, where each Saturday women with straw-bundle brooms emerge from virtually every house to attack the already spotless cobbles before them and where each Sunday morning men gather in dark, smoky inns to gossip, drink beer, and play cards.

Along the Altmühl and its tributaries stand communities that look as if they have been lifted whole from a medieval print—places like Berching, where colorful half-timbered houses jostle along narrow lanes within an encircling town wall, its dozen towers and

More than a dozen countries will gain access to 7,000 miles of inland waterways.

Water from the Danube system will be transported to northern Bavaria, where it will be held in reservoirs such as the Rothsee for release into the canal and into the Main during periods of low water.

A diver with a video camera checks for cracks in Leerstetten lock, which raises ships seven stories to the next lock level.

gatehouses as sturdy as when they were built more than 500 years ago, or Prunn, whose inhabitants have been sheltered through the centuries beneath one of the most dramatically overbearing castles in Europe. In such places the distance to metropolises like Munich and Nürnberg is measured not in miles but in years.

With its neighboring valleys, the Altmühl forms the largest *Naturpark,* or protected area, in Germany. The idea of driving a 180-foot-wide canal through such a timeless and

BILL BRYSON is an Iowa-born journalist now living in North Yorkshire, England. His article on "The New World of Spain" appeared in the April 1992 GEOGRAPHIC. Los Angeles-based photographer GERD LUDWIG covered his native country in the September 1991 article "The Morning After: Germany Reunited."

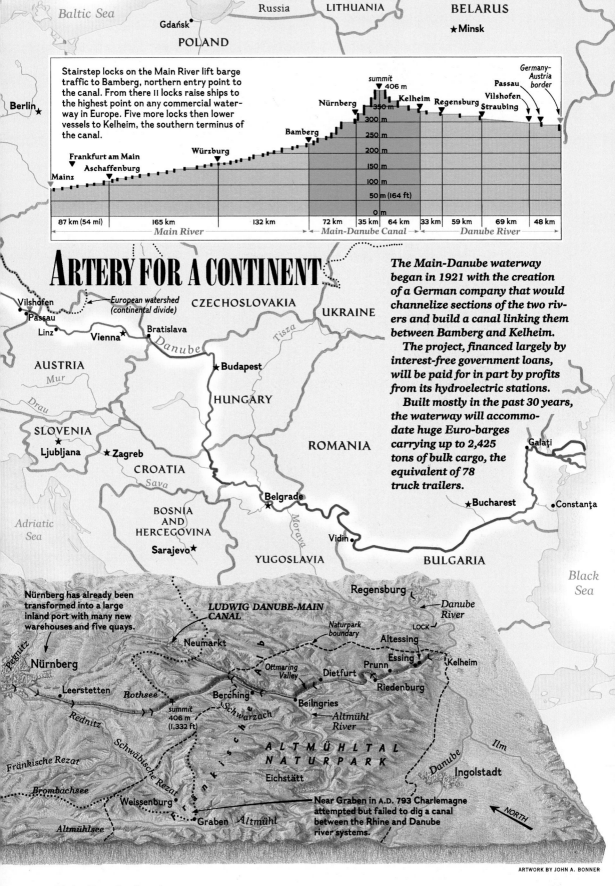

ARTERY FOR A CONTINENT

Stairstep locks on the Main River lift barge traffic to Bamberg, northern entry point to the canal. From there 11 locks raise ships to the highest point on any commercial waterway in Europe. Five more locks then lower vessels to Kelheim, the southern terminus of the canal.

summit 406 m

Germany-Austria border

| 87 km (54 mi) | 165 km | 132 km | 72 km | 35 km | 64 km | 33 km | 59 km | 69 km | 48 km |

Main River — Main-Danube Canal — Danube River

The Main-Danube waterway began in 1921 with the creation of a German company that would channelize sections of the two rivers and build a canal linking them between Bamberg and Kelheim.

The project, financed largely by interest-free government loans, will be paid for in part by profits from its hydroelectric stations.

Built mostly in the past 30 years, the waterway will accommodate huge Euro-barges carrying up to 2,425 tons of bulk cargo, the equivalent of 78 truck trailers.

Nürnberg has already been transformed into a large inland port with many new warehouses and five quays.

LUDWIG DANUBE-MAIN CANAL

Naturpark boundary

Near Graben in A.D. 793 Charlemagne attempted but failed to dig a canal between the Rhine and Danube river systems.

ALTMÜHLTAL NATURPARK

European watershed (continental divide)

ARTWORK BY JOHN A. BONNER

dreamy landscape has been, understandably, a cause of some disquiet.

"I thought it would break my heart," Walter Spiegler, a retired veterinarian in Beilngries, told me. An amateur ornithologist, Spiegler first came to the Altmühl Valley in 1957, attracted in large part by its untrampled remoteness and abundant birdlife. "I used to see whinchats and bluethroats every few paces. Now I am lucky to see a single pair in a day. Instead I see bulldozers. Naturally that makes me sad."

Or as Ludwig Bauer, a dentist and town councilman in Eichstätt, put it: "It is harder and harder to find a natural landscape in Germany. We keep clawing away at it. Eventually there will be nothing left."

Yet others are enthusiastic. "Riedenburg, where I went to school, was becoming a

terrible mess," says Gerlinde Chloupek, who now lives in Eichstätt. "The canal has attracted tourists and that in turn has prompted businesspeople to make improvements. So the whole thing has acted as a kind of catalyst. It has transformed the town."

THOUGH THE SCALE is vastly more ambitious now, this is not the first time a canal has been built through the Altmühl Valley. In 1837, King Ludwig I of Bavaria put a corps of laborers to work digging a navigable trench between Bamberg and Kelheim that took in much of the route of today's waterway. The Ludwig Danube-Main Canal was completed in 1845, but the king didn't even bother to attend the opening ceremony.

The canal operated for a century in a mostly

desultory and loss-making fashion, unable to compete effectively with the new railways and left idle for long periods by low water in the Main. With locks only 16 feet wide, the canal was also plagued by the problem of having to transfer goods from wide river barges to narrow canalboats.

"The accounts of the time show that the operators of the canal made more money by selling fishing rights and renting out orchards and farmland along the banks than they made from the canal," says Dieter Häckl, director of Regensburg harbor, just beyond the new canal's southern end at Kelheim. With a wry smile he adds: "I trust that that will not be the case this time."

In 1921, under the auspices of the federal and Bavarian state governments, a company was formed to build a replacement canal on a

Protected from flying gravel, a woman watches construction at Berching. The canal was slowed in the early 1980s by rising costs and environmental protests. One government minister called it "the most stupid project since the Tower of Babel." In the Ottmaring Valley (left) and elsewhere a total of 130 million cubic yards of earth was moved.

far grander scale. Apart from a hiatus after the Second World War, the firm of Rhein-Main-Donau AG (RMD) has spent the past 70 years building the waterway piece by piece, first improving the channels of both the Main and the Danube. It also has erected 55 hydroelectric power stations (the number will eventually rise to 60).

"Seventy years is a long time to realize a

dream, but at last we seem to be there," Hans Peter Seidel, a managing director of RMD, tells me in his office in Munich, where I have come to meet him and manager Jens Friese.

Seidel is clearly proud of the achievement and has no doubt about the need for the new waterway. "Transporting bulk goods by water is cheaper, cleaner, and more energy efficient than by any other means," he points out. He shows me an article from that morning's paper about a study of the comparative costs of moving freight in Germany. According to the study, to move one ton of goods one kilometer costs 14 pfennigs (about nine cents) by rail and 29 pfennigs by road, but just 4 pfennigs by inland waterway. "And that study, please note," Seidel adds with a smile that borders on the mischievous, "was conducted on behalf of the state railway."

Friese reels off the canal's many other benefits. It will act as an economic spur to the region. It will provide flood control. It will allow the transfer of water from southern Bavaria and the Altmühl Valley, where

Precision engineering placed the canal only 80 feet from Berching without destabilizing the town's medieval walls (opposite). The raw cut at left, now a sports field, will be the scene of canal opening ceremonies on September 25.

To conceal concrete banks, workers (above) set local stones in asphalt. A worker (top) takes a last look at the drainage system under the canal bed before sealing the access hole.

The project also includes roads, bridges, hydroelectric plants, and reservoirs.

supplies are plentiful, to water-poor northern Bavaria. It will dilute pollution in the Main by pumping in cleaner water from the Danube. And it will provide recreational opportunities both along the canal and on several new artificial lakes. "These incidental benefits are in many ways as important as the canal itself," Friese says.

Best of all, according to Seidel, the whole is self-financing. Profits from the power stations —55 million marks (about 34 million dollars) a year—underwrite much of the expense of construction. The rest is made up largely through interest-free loans from the federal government and the state of Bavaria. "But these," Seidel says, "will be paid back in full by the year 2050, when the power stations will be turned over to them."

As the two men cheerfully admit, it sounds almost too good to be true. So why, I ask, has the canal project encountered such fervent opposition? "The canal became a symbol for protesters," Friese tells me. "For the most part, the protests didn't come from people living near the canal. They came from people in cities like Hamburg and Munich. Many of the early critics didn't even know where the Altmühl Valley was."

Concerned about the protests as well as

mounting costs for the project, the federal government withdrew its support in 1982. "They allowed us to complete what we were building but wouldn't permit us to start new works," Friese recalls. "But we never believed it would be permanently stopped, because, of course, it would be nonsense to build half a canal and then leave it."

The election of a more sympathetic administration under Helmut Kohl allowed the project to continue. RMD insists that it was sensitive to environmental concerns before the protests began but concedes that the brush with failure sharpened its resolve to make the canal as undisturbing as possible.

THIS CHANGE IN ATTITUDE is strikingly evident as you travel south along the canal past the old cities of Bamberg and Nürnberg and up through the long, windy plateau of the Fränkische Alb. Here, 1,332 feet above sea level, the highest point of any commercial waterway in Europe, the canal is straight, functional, and businesslike—impressive but charmless. But as it descends into the Altmühl Valley, it takes on a sudden and often startling beauty. It looks not like a canal but like a river— stately, winding, varied in width, its sloping banks crowded with foliage, its backwaters teeming with birds.

The credit for this transformation belongs almost entirely to a genial and farsighted landscape architect named Reinhard Grebe. With 20 enthusiastic young assistants, Grebe works in an atmosphere of controlled chaos in an office on a back street in Nürnberg, just around the corner from St. Johannis Cemetery, the resting-place of artist Albrecht Dürer and many of the city's other luminaries.

"In 1972," Grebe says, pushing back a shock of hair and seizing a pencil with which he produces a series of rapid sketches, "RMD asked me to make a landscape plan for the lower Altmühl Valley. They wanted me to deal with only the five-meter-strip of land on either side of the canal, like so. But I insisted on looking at the whole of the valley. This had never

Excavating ahead of the bulldozers, archaeologists found this skull amid a thousand Celtic burials they identified, including the largest Celtic graveyard in Bavaria. Grave goods point to social stratification among farmers of 600 B.C.

been done before—landscape architecture was traditionally regarded as a kind of afterthought, and I think they were shocked, but to their credit they let me go ahead."

Grebe brought in experts from every relevant discipline—climatologists, biologists, zoologists, town planners, an ichthyologist, some 20 people in all—and drew up a radical scheme for the valley. "The original plans were terrible," Grebe recalls. "The engineers wanted to make the canal straight and build roads down both sides of it. It would have destroyed the valley utterly. We insisted that they make the canal look more natural, that they give it backwaters for the protection of wildlife, that they keep one side free of traffic and build a bikeway instead, and many other things. It meant they had to tear up their plans and start again." And how was this received? Grebe smiles. "With rage and fury," he says.

Particular care was given to preserving stretches of the old canal (much of which had been bombed into oblivion during the Second World War) and to creating "biotopes" along the new canal's edge—areas of still water protected from the waves of passing ships by levees of rock—to encourage the resettlement of birds and other wildlife.

"It took a long time to change people's attitudes," Grebe remembers. "In the 1970s there was no tradition in Germany of looking at the environmental impact of a project. In much of the world there still isn't, I'm sorry to say, so in this sense I think we can allow ourselves a little pride."

Nonetheless he retains deep misgivings about the canal. "Yes, on the whole I wish it hadn't been built. However good a job we did, there is no escaping the fact that now there is a large canal where once there was a small, beautiful river and a small, unobtrusive canal. Sometimes I blame myself. If we hadn't drawn up such a good plan, maybe the canal wouldn't have been allowed."

"I was once walking along the canal," Ernst Reinhold of RMD tells me, "and I overheard some tourists saying, 'Isn't it a shame that they are going to destroy this beautiful valley for the sake of a canal?' What these people didn't realize was that they were looking at a finished portion of the canal. Most people can't tell the difference, you see. The Altmühl Valley was beautiful before, and it is beautiful still."

We are standing on the bridge of the *Seidlstein,* an icebreaker on a training run from Regensburg to Riedenburg, and I am unable to disagree with him. Partly this is because he is right—it *is* beautiful—but also because I am preoccupied with the unsettling discovery that it is entirely possible to get seasick 500 miles from the sea. The *Seidlstein* is proceeding up the canal in a manner reminiscent of a rocking horse. Gerhard Pavel, the captain, explains that when the ice is very thick, as it is today, the only way to break it is to rock the ship over it, repeatedly hurling the vessel forward and allowing its sheer weight to fracture the ice as the ship—and with it my stomach—falls heavily forward. It is a tricky operation and takes some practice. Hence this run. Hence also my creeping queasiness.

Fortunately a little beyond Kelheim the ice thins, and we resume a stately evenness of progress. Even on a frosty January morning the canal is fetching almost beyond words. Herons sweep along the *Altwasser*—the

At Essing, planks bonded by glue form a footbridge that undulates like a wave. Bridges in the Altmühl region were architect-designed, and each is different. Seven of the lockhouses built by King Ludwig's architect were preserved.

stretches of old water from the Altmühl River and Ludwig canal that have been preserved as oxbows and side channels—and villages that seem untouched by time slide past on the rolling banks on either side. Apart from a few intrusions of bare earth where the finishing touches are being put on bridges or biotopes, the canal and the Altmühl look as if they have happily coexisted for eons rather than—in some places—as little as a couple of years.

"We didn't stint," Reinhold notes. He is a chief engineer for RMD, but his work these days is concerned as much with aesthetics as with nuts and bolts and flow rates.

"So far, we have spent 280 million marks [173 million dollars] on landscaping," Reinhold goes on, "which I think is more than on any other comparable project in the world.

And we took unusual pains with almost every other aspect. Along this stretch, for instance, you will notice that every bridge is different. We did that intentionally, to avoid monotony. Instead of buying ready-made plans from engineering firms, we employed architects to design bridges that are beautiful as well as functional. It cost much more, but it was well worth it."

Perhaps nowhere was this extra care realized more successfully than at Essing, where a novel wooden footbridge, the longest in Europe, stretches 630 feet across the canal. Designed by Munich architect Richard J. Dietrich and built in the shape of two lazy waves, it looks disarmingly like some cunningly recycled section of the Coney Island roller coaster. It is impossible, I had been told, to walk across its languorous rises and

Leading his flock to evening shelter, shepherd Karl Schwarz walks grassy embankments he leases for "too much." Yet his share weighs small given the 4.2-billion-dollar price tag of the project.

the canal; not everyone believed they would fulfill them, but they did. We have new bridges, which are much sturdier than the old ones, and a wonderful new sportsground. You should go and see it."

I DID, and I appreciated his enthusiasm. With a floodlighted soccer field, tennis courts, an all-weather running track, and a well-appointed clubhouse, the sportsground was lavish beyond the dreams of most rural hamlets. Up and down the valley I found other towns and villages boasting new parks or sportsgrounds and residents pleased to point them out.

"We try very hard to make everyone happy," Alois Pröll tells me a few days later. Pröll is a site manager for the canal between Riedenburg and Dietfurt. This is his first job since earning his engineering degree, and he loves every minute of it. "I would probably work for free—but don't put that in your article, because my boss might read it," he says as we climb into a four-wheel-drive vehicle for a tour of his ten-mile domain. He has the quick and casual wit of a native Bavarian. When I observe uneasily at one point that we are going 80 kilometers (50 miles) per hour in a 40 kph zone, he replies, "Oh, that's OK— there are two of us."

He speeds us past platoons of bulldozers digging out the last of the 130 million cubic yards of earth to make the canal and fondly points out the improvements that RMD has made to the valley—waterside walks, restored lockhouses, a new farmhouse for a family whose property stood uncomfortably near the site of a new bridge, a landing for pleasure craft.

Pröll nods at a vast rectangular mound of recently excavated black earth. "That's 40,000 cubic meters of humus, very rich soil. We pile it there and let the farmers help themselves, and, of course, they are very pleased to get this good soil for nothing. The rest of it we take up into the hills and distribute to the farmers up there, and they are very grateful because their land isn't so good. So you see almost everyone benefits."

falls without feeling a huge, childlike impulse to break into a gallop (a fact I confirmed, with a sense of helpless astonishment, the next day).

Reinhold points to the village of Essing, nestled between a stretch of the old canal and an almost perpendicular hill at its back. "The highway through the valley used to go through the village. Now the road bypasses Essing, so it is quieter and safer for the residents. You see, we didn't just build a canal. We transformed the valley. In almost every way we made life better for the people who live here."

"Yes, I would agree with that," Peter Ehrl, proprietor of a restaurant in the neighboring village of Altessing, tells me later. "Before they started construction, RMD made many promises to the villages along

Coal from South Africa, 2,800 tons loaded on a two-unit convoy in Rotterdam, travels under a Main River bridge to Bamberg. The Väth company

foresees an unlimited future for bulk transport via the canal. Hungary,
for instance, may order United States coal for electric plants.

Pröll drops me at Berching lock, half a mile from the walled town from which it takes its name and, at the time of my visit, one of the last unfinished locks on the canal.

Filled with water, a lock is impressive; empty it is simply awesome. Each lock chamber on the Main-Danube Canal is 625 feet long, 40 feet wide, and up to 100 feet deep. To stand at the bottom of the chamber staring up at almost 200,000 cubic yards of concrete—with walls as high as an eight-story building—you have a sudden humbled sense of what it must feel like to be an ant in a bathtub. Yet this vast chamber, holding 10.5 million gallons of water, can be filled in just 20 minutes.

T HE LOCK LOOKS BIG ENOUGH to accommodate a flotilla, but in fact a single one of the latest generation of barges fits it as snugly as an arm in a sleeve. These Euro-barges, carrying up to 2,425 tons of freight, almost always in the form of low-value bulk goods like coal, sand, or grain, can stretch as long as 200 yards, with a beam up to 38 feet, leaving a bare 12 inches of maneuvering room on each side.

Even for older, smaller barges, it can be a heartstoppingly tight squeeze, as I discovered when I spent a day aboard the working barge M.S. *Hünenkönig (King of Giants)* traveling south from Bamberg to Nürnberg as a guest of Dirk and Chirley Breidenbach and their six-year-old son, Steven.

The Breidenbachs, from Germany, are one of the scores of families who lead an engagingly rootless life traveling the waterways of Europe, conveying freight from one inland port to another, living aboard their ships. At the time of my visit in April 1991, they were taking 680 tons of fertilizer to Nürnberg, having dropped 550 tons of sunflower seeds at Würzburg two days before. At Nürnberg the shipping agency for which they work would provide them with new orders that could take them to any of several dozen far-flung places—to Amsterdam, Rotterdam, Frankfurt, Nancy, Mannheim.

By modern standards, the 40-year-old *Hünenkönig* is relatively small at 280 feet

Piloted with finesse, the Väth coal convoy, equipped with electronic controls, eases its 30-foot beam into the 40-foot-wide lock at Wipfeld on the Main (left). Romanian boatman Mitică Mihalcea, with family aboard, steers his aging barge on the Danube. Lacking an engine, the vessel must be towed by a tugboat.

long and 30 feet broad, but the operative word here is "relatively." From the bridge, the low, metal-roofed storage holds stretch out before us for what seems like an eternity. When Chirley goes forward to make coffee in the galley, she becomes little more than a distant dot. Yet Dirk maneuvers this ungainly behemoth with consummate ease, slipping her into each lock as casually as if posting a letter, while at the same time talking on the shortwave, dealing patiently with a sleeve-tugging question from Steven, and searching for his cigarettes among the charts and clutter beside the steering mechanism.

It is not an easy life. The Breidenbachs rise at five and keep the ship moving 14 hours a day. With no other crew to help them, they often work seven or eight days at a stretch. But the *Hünenkönig* is not without its comforts. The living quarters boast all the vital appurtenances of modern life—VCR, stereo system, microwave oven, even a satellite dish. The ship carries the family car too, for weekly trips to the supermarket. "There isn't anything families on land have that we haven't got here—except, of course, a backyard," says Chirley as she shows me around. Or, it occurs to me, a mailbox. What do the Breidenbachs do for mail?

"Oh, we have it delivered to the lockhouse at Kostheim," Chirley says airily. "We pass through there every few weeks."

She finds nothing odd in living without a permanent address, but this is perhaps not surprising. Chirley grew up on a barge— indeed was born on a barge—and has always lived like this. Dirk by comparison is a land-lubber—he has spent only about half his 29 years on boats—but, like Chirley, he cannot now conceive of any other kind of life.

"It's so peaceful on the water. Once you have experienced that, it is very hard to go back," he says. "I know it must seem odd to be constantly moving from place to place and not having a permanent home. But to me to wake up every day and see the same view out the window—now that would seem odd."

The one drawback to waterborne family life is that children from the age of six have to be shipped off to special boarding schools for ten months of the year. "It can be an awful wrench," says Chirley. Steven will soon face the experience for the first time—though at least he will be in the company of his older brother, Jens, who has been away for two years, returning to the boat only for school holidays and the occasional weekend.

Steven professes to be eager to go, but he looks awfully small for such a big step. I ask him if he would like to work on a barge like this one day, and he gives me one of those looks that small children reserve for dangerously stupid adults. "I already do," he informs me simply. I decide that he will do well at school.

ONE OF THE NOTABLE THINGS is how little other traffic we see—two coal barges moored at a power station on the outskirts of Nürnberg and one other barge chugging past in the other direction. Partly, Dirk explains, it is because it is a quiet time of year and also because Nürnberg is a dead end. When the rest of the canal opens in September 1992, connecting Nürnberg and the north to the Danube and beyond, the traffic will almost certainly increase. "But there is no guarantee that it will be huge," Dirk says. "It may still be quiet along here. No one knows."

Possibly the most remarkable fact about the Main-Danube Canal project is that no one appears to know quite how much it has cost. Hans Peter Seidel of RMD told me in Munich that the cumulative outlay since 1921 was "about seven billion marks" (4.2 billion dollars), but even he conceded that that was at constant, unadjusted prices—the purchasing power of one mark in 1921 was obviously quite different from the value of one mark today—and no one apparently has ever computed the real cost of extending interest-free loans to RMD over a period of seven decades.

What is certain is that many people believe that the canal, whatever the final cost, will never pay its way. To find out why, I went to the University of Erlangen-Nürnberg to see Eugen Wirth, a slight, sprightly, white-haired man who can only be described as engagingly feisty. You must get up early to catch Professor Wirth—his working day starts at 5:30 a.m.

"Before 9 a.m. you can do your work.

After 9 a.m. you are *being* worked!" he explains in a good-natured bellow. Wirth has been studying Germany's waterways since 1952. Waterborne freight is an important component of Germany's transportation network, carrying about a fourth of all freight, and Wirth is an enthusiast for the system. But for the new Main-Danube Canal he has scarcely a good word.

"It is completely unnecessary—an extravagant folly! People forget that there already *is* a route between the North Sea and Black Sea—the Atlantic and Mediterranean. It is ten times cheaper to take freight by sea because the ships are ten times bigger and they move faster. Barges on the waterway will have to negotiate many locks—more than 50 between Frankfurt and Passau alone, and on the canal itself there is a speed limit of 11

kilometers an hour. It will take on average 23 to 30 days to get from the North Sea to the Black Sea by inland waterway, against just six days by sea. Where is the economic sense in that?"

RMD counters that the canal was built to expand inland trade, not to compete for sea-to-sea traffic. Wirth estimates that in order to be profitable the Main-Danube Canal would need to see trade of 22 million to 27 million tons a year—far beyond even RMD's most optimistic forecasts. In the mid-1980s RMD was predicting as much as 11 million tons of traffic—Wirth believes three million tons is a more likely figure—but now declines to offer even informal forecasts. The company argues that political changes in Eastern Europe have made projections impossible but that trade along the canal will almost certainly boom as a result.

Wirth thinks not. "The economies of Eastern Europe are in disarray, and it is unlikely that they will be significant customers of Western bulk goods for many years. At the same time, we in Western Europe have chronic surpluses of grain and other agricultural produce and don't need what they have to offer. So I ask you: Where will the trade come from?"

MANY ENVIRONMENTALISTS are equally unconvinced of the canal's merits. "Mere landscape cosmetics" is how Klaus Giessner, a professor of physical geography at the Catholic University of Eichstätt, characterizes RMD's efforts in the Altmühl Valley. "Superficially it may look attractive, but the natural dynamism is being destroyed and that cannot be replaced."

Nor does Giessner accept many of the arguments concerning the canal's incidental benefits. "The transfer of water to the north could have been achieved with a small pipeline. You don't need a large canal for that. As to pollution in the Main, surely it would

Water over the bridge carries traffic high above the Zenn River (top). Headed back to their Romanian home with a cargo of German logs, the Mihalcea family turns barge decks into a make-do playground. The used car they bought in Germany gains in value with every mile it floats down the Danube River.

Sunday picnic by a reflecting pool—a newly completed section of canal—appeals to Turkish guest worker Mehmet Aldogan, at right.

*He, his friends, and their families travel 12 miles from Neumarkt to
share food and strong hot tea in the country.*

make more sense to clean the water than merely dilute it.

"The question of flood control," he goes on, "is more problematic. From a social point of view, flooding is, of course, a bad thing. But from an environmental point of view it has certain virtues. It permits the existence of water meadows on which many species of plants and animals depend. More crucially, the drying up of meadows means that farmers are now able to cultivate them

Waiting for his beer to cool, a swimmer relaxes beside his campsite near Leerstetten lock. These waters may not be peaceful for long. Anticipating the canal's opening, pleasure boaters plan new cruises, farmers look forward to expanded markets, and nations seek increased waterborne trade.

intensively. We are already seeing critically high concentrations of nitrates in the canal—and this is before it has even opened."

Peter Herre, an environmentalist for the state of Bavaria, has found more than two dozen species of plants and animals whose existence in the valley he feels may be seriously threatened—birds like the meadow pipit and blue-headed wagtail, insects like the dragonfly and damselfly, and many kinds of flora, from marsh orchids to gingerbread sedge.

"We can't tell for certain which species will adapt and survive," he says. "We won't know that for five or ten or maybe even fifteen years, but by then it will be too late."

Herre has a particular reason for feeling strongly about the canal. He has lived in the Altmühl Valley all his life. "It's true that tourists sometimes come and say, 'Oh, it looks very nice,' but they don't know what

it was like before. It was idyllic, totally unspoiled, with a beautiful little river and an unusually rich variety of wildlife. All that has been lost for the sake of a waterway that is environmentally unsound and, in all likelihood, economically pointless."

THE IMPRESSION of almost universal disdain among environmentalists and academics is inescapable. Even Bernd Engelhardt, whose work has been unquestionably aided by the canal, would rather it had never been built. A large, friendly man, Dr. Engelhardt is the head of archaeology for southeastern Bavaria. From a scholarly point of view, the canal has been a windfall to him.

"The Altmühl Valley is very rich in artifacts," he says as he shows me around his headquarters in Landshut, where workers in

white coats patiently transform clumps of dirt and oddments of encrusted iron into gleaming and recognizable objects like knives and brooches. "We found a great deal there—a more or less complete settlement every two to three kilometers. Since 1975, when our work began, we have collected more than a million items. It will take us probably 20 years to catalog them all."

We stop for a moment to watch two women rebuilding large earthen pots from a box of loose fragments, many of them no larger than a baby's thumbnail. How long does it take to rebuild a pot? "Oh, about six months," one of the women tells me, looking not the least bit depressed.

"We had an arrangement with RMD," Engelhardt continues, "whereby they would tell us where they were going to dig next and give us six months to get in ahead of them. They also voluntarily gave us money, which is *very* unusual, believe me. And I have to say they continue to give generously—over half a million marks a year. We couldn't have done it without them."

"And yet," I ask, puzzled, "you would rather the canal had not been built?"

Engelhardt gives me a frank smile. "Sometimes it was a little like gold fever, you know? As an archaeologist it was very exciting. But that doesn't mean that I am in favor of despoiling large sections of landscape simply so that I can have the pleasure of picking through interesting old objects. Yes, I wish the canal had not been built."

On my last afternoon in the Altmühl Valley I went to the footbridge at Essing for a final look at the canal. I decided—lamely, I confess—that I couldn't make up my mind about it. Without the benefit of knowing the valley before the canal, it was impossible to tell how seriously its rhythms and appearance have been disrupted. It seems an obvious pity to tinker with nature for the sake of a project that may never be economically justified. On the other hand, there is no denying that RMD has taken extraordinary pains to make the canal fit the landscape. As the sun tracked its way toward the hills to my left and the day's last tractors labored home across the neat fields, I couldn't help reflecting that it looked as if it had been there forever.

Which is, of course, a merciful thing because, for better or worse, it will be there forever now. ☐

STRUGGLE OF THE

By CHRISTOPHER HITCHENS

KURDS

Fleeing their war-torn home near Kirkuk, Iraq, a Kurdish family clings to life in the ruins of Panjwin, on the border with Iran. Without a nation of their own, the Kurds live, as they have lived for centuries, at the mercy of powerful and often hostile neighbors.

Photographs by ED KASHI

For time out of mind, Kurdish women have filled their water jars in Qalat Dizah, Iraq. The modern city lies in rubble, dynamited and bulldozed by Iraqi troops in 1989.

Since the mid-1970s President Saddam Hussein's campaign
to eradicate the Kurdish resistance movement has claimed
4,000 towns and villages and more than 100,000 lives.

35

IF YOU TAKE A PLANE from Istanbul and fly southeastward to Diyarbakir, you stay in the same country. But you leave Europe for the Middle East, and you enter the world of the Kurds. In Diyarbakir, a boiling, teeming city enclosed within ancient walls made of forbidding black basalt, the Kurdish flag is prohibited and use of the Kurdish language restricted. So elevator boys and waiters were being careful when whispering to Westerners like myself: "This is not Turkey... this is Kurdistan. Diyarbakır—*capital* of Kurdistan.... We are not Turks... we are Kurds."

I visited a coffee shop with my new friend Hasan, a young Kurd who had agreed to show me his city. I watched as he looked around in disgust through the plumes of tobacco haze and took the proprietor to one side. Within seconds the loud cassette music had been replaced by another tape, more wild and mournful sounding—but not until

the boss had cast a swift glance down the street. Taking the best table, Hasan—a man of relatively few words—explained: "Stupid Turkish music. I told him play some good Kurdish tunes."

I had come in search of the Kurds, a people who in 1991 had been abruptly and cruelly promoted to center stage by their battle against Saddam Hussein's regime and by the sympathy felt in the West for those who had suffered longer than the Kuwaitis from Saddam's ambitions. For months I would travel among them, trying to make sense of where this ancient people fit in the modern world.

Who are the Kurds? They number 25 million and are scattered from the Middle East to Europe, North America, and Australia, which makes them one of the largest ethnic groups in the world without a state of its own. Once nomadic, most are now farmers or have migrated to cities.

Like the majority of their neighbors, most Kurds are Sunni Muslims; a few are Jews or Christians. Their language is fractured—like the Kurds themselves—by region and dialect, but it is distinct from Turkish, Persian, and Arabic. They are neither Turks, nor Persians, nor Arabs, and they regard their own survival as proof in itself of a certain integrity.

For more than 2,000 years, travelers to the heart of Kurdish country have reported on the blue or green eyes and fair hair seen among the Kurds—and on their fierceness. Four centuries before Christ, as the Greeks were retreating from the Persians toward the Black Sea, Xenophon recorded that they were harassed along the way by Kardouchoi, people who "dwelt up among the mountains . . . a warlike people . . . not subjects of the King." Most modern scholars agree that this is a reference to the Kurds.

Some three million Kurds live in the region of Iraq they call Free Kurdistan, in the mountains where Turkey, Iran, Syria, and Iraq come together. Here, since the humbling of Saddam, the Kurds have established the largest and most populous area of autonomy in their modern history: an area of some 15,000 square miles where Kurds are giving orders, collecting taxes, holding rudimentary courts, and conducting their own parliamentary elections, primarily between the two major parties, Jalal Talabani's Patriotic Union of Kurdistan and Masoud Barzani's Kurdistan Democratic Party. But the Kurds seldom

Kurdish separatists in Turkey launched a violent new offensive this spring.

In 1945 Iranian Kurds declared the independent Republic of Mahabad, which lasted one year.

After the gulf war Western forces established a security zone north of the 36th parallel to encourage the return of Kurdish refugees to Iraq.

In 1987 and 1988 Iraqis attacked Kurdish villages, including Halabjah, with cyanide and mustard gas.

Birthplace of medieval Kurdish hero Saladin and modern Kurdish nemesis Saddam Hussein.

Area of Kurdish predominance

Oil field

0   100 km
0   100 mi

NGS CARTOGRAPHIC DIVISION

Map labels:

Black Sea · Caspian Sea · CAUCASUS MOUNTAINS · GEORGIA · RUSSIA · 5,033 m · Batumi · Tbilisi · Trabzon · ARMENIA · AZERBAIJAN · Yerevan · Sivas · Erzincan · Erzurum · Euphrates · Mt. Ararat 5,137 m 16,854 ft · NAKHICHEVAN (AZERBAIJAN) · Aras · TURKEY · +3,250 m · Karlıova · Elâzığ · Muş · 4,434 m · Lake Van · Van · Khvoy · Malatya · Murat · Adıyaman · Atatürk Dam · Diyarbakır · Tigris · 3,610 m · Tabriz · Lake Urmia · K U R D I S T A N · Işıkveren (refugee camp) · Cizre · Zakhu · Urmia · Urfa · Al Qamishli · Dahuk · Rawanduz · Mahabad · IRAN · Great Zab · +1,519 m · Mosul · Shaqlawah · Khalifan · 36TH PARALLEL · Arbil · Qalat Dizah · Dayr az Zawr · Khabur · M E S O P O T A M I A · Little Zab · Panjwin · As Sulaymaniyah · Sanandaj · Kirkuk · Halabjah · SYRIA · I R A Q · +3,366 m · Diyala R. · Tharthar Lake · Tikrit · Kermanshah · Zagros Mts. · Baghdad · Simareh · Babylon · Tigris · Dezful · JORDAN

CONFRONTATION IN KURDISTAN

Kurds have occupied the sweep of mountains and foothills northeast of Mesopotamia since ancient times. Rich in oil and water, the region called Kurdistan assumed its modern borders after World War I, the arbitrary partitions compounding existing religious and linguistic divisions among Kurds.

Now 25 million strong, Kurds constitute one of the largest ethnic groups in the world without a country of its own. This political vulnerability prompted two million Iraqi Kurds to flee their homes for camps like Işıkveren, Turkey (opposite), when the uprising against Saddam Hussein failed after the gulf war.

Black Sea · RUSSIA · Istanbul · Caspian Sea · GEORGIA · ARMENIA · AZERBAIJAN · ★Ankara · TURKEY · Anatolia · IRAN · Beirut · SYRIA · Bekaa Valley · LEBANON · Damascus · IRAQ · Mediterranean Sea · ISRAEL · Jerusalem ★ · AREA ENLARGED · EGYPT · JORDAN · KUWAIT · SAUDI ARABIA · Persian Gulf · 0 250 km · 0 250 mi

Lives hang in the balance as Sabry Ahmed cradles her son Howkar in what is left of Qalat Dizah. The Iraqi government has imposed a strict blockade of food and fuel to the region known as Free Kurdistan, where families struggle to rebuild amid the wreckage. Children of Panjwin study in a freezing warren of debris that remained after shelling by the Iraqi Army in the 1970s.

speak with one voice; indeed the positions of the two parties have often shifted. Today the central issues are: Should the Kurds sign a limited autonomy agreement with Saddam (the Barzani view) or should they hold out for more territory and more political concessions (the Talabani position)?

When I arrived in Free Kurdistan, in the spring of 1991, there was a swath of trouble and grief on every side. To the south, Saddam's forces were mustering again to reassert central control. To the north, the Turkish authorities maintained that Turkey was one nation and that Kurds were part of the Turkish family. To the east, the Kurds of Iran chafed under the rule of the mullahs as they had under the shah. To the west, in Syria, the Kurds were some distance from full citizenship; in Lebanon and beyond they were in diaspora.

The Kurds have survived like other large minorities, by sniffing the wind and being adroit at the business of tactics. While in large parts of the West the Kurds are hailed as tough, romantic, and dashing, it isn't unusual to hear them described by their immediate neighbors as downright uncouth, oil greedy, and for sale to the highest bidder.

To the impatient, proud regional powers that already enjoy statehood, the Kurds are *in the way*. In the way of Saddam's dream of a greater Babylon, glory of the Arabs. In the way of Turkey's plan to earn international respect by modernizing and assimilating the Kurdish provinces. In the way of Iran's scheme for a republic based on Shiite Islam. In the way of Syria's wish to make a militarized nation out of a patchwork of religious and ethnic minorities.

The Kurdish national motto, with origins older than anyone can remember, is simply: "The Kurds have no friends."

IN THE MONTHS just after the gulf war ended in March 1991 it was still dangerous to visit Iraqi Kurdistan, so I enlisted the help of an armed escort hardened by months of guerrilla fighting. Hoshyar Samsam, who knew this country well and had been the personal bodyguard of Jalal Talabani, was taking care of me. He calmly conducted me through bomb-shattered villages and deserted towns. He foraged for me in an area blighted by

famine and helped me dodge Iraqi patrols. He looked as if he could carry me if the need arose, and I wasn't sure it might not. He had a fierce, beaming face and huge hands. His hair was reddish and his eyes blue-green. I asked him to tell me his story.

Hoshyar was born to a peasant family in the hills near Kirkuk, the oil capital of Iraqi Kurdistan. He had been brought up on ancestral tales of Kurdish suffering and defiance and had carried this formative memory with him when he left home for Baghdad to study engineering.

In the great Kurdish uprising that followed Desert Storm, Hoshyar was an enthusiastic

British journalist, critic, and essayist CHRISTOPHER HITCHENS is the Washington, D. C., editor for *Harper's* magazine and a columnist for *The Nation*. This is his first article for the GEOGRAPHIC.

militant, and a photograph of President George Bush in a jogging outfit was gummed proudly to the windshield of his Toyota jeep. After the first exhilarating days of the revolution—"We took our great city of Kirkuk, without any help from anyone"—he had been caught up in the defeat, exodus, and massacre that captured world attention.

"What about your family?" I asked.

Hoshyar's answer was slightly shrugging. He is a *peshmerga*—in the Kurdish term of honor, one who has made an understanding with death. He was married to the struggle and had no time for domesticity. His relatives were extended all over the hills of the area and scattered between the refugee camps and shelters that dot Iraqi Kurdistan today. "Maybe, after victory, I have my own family."

The Kurds might well have broken and

*Iraqi Kurdish guerrillas called **peshmerga** take lessons in mortar fire and single-file patrol near a captured military base. Although many Kurdish men have spent a lifetime under arms, their equipment, training, and numbers are no match for the best of the modern Iraqi Army.*

dispersed by now if it weren't for the strength of their family tradition. Everyone seems related to everyone else; it's also sometimes true. Cousins, for example, are encouraged to marry so that farms and orchards can stay in the family. In the squares and streets, men would keep asking photographer Ed Kashi to take pictures of their children. The Kurdish family is the nexus of their solidarity and survival. Even this, though, is linked to "the struggle." An old man we met in the village of Khalifan was sitting with his submachine gun hung over the back of a chair and watching his grandsons frisking about. When I praised their charm and friendliness, he beamed. "Yes," he said. "They will make good soldiers."

Even among the Kurds who live in seemingly normal circumstances, there are the daily reminders of reality.

In the old city of Diyarbakır, for instance, a foreign visitor can leave the noise and smoke of the street, pass through thick walls opening on to a shaded courtyard, and settle in at one of 20 tables at the Trafik Çay Bahçesı, a tea garden. Children play on brightly painted swings and slides nearby. Young men and women hold hands, chat, and loll away the warm autumn afternoon over bottled Coke or small glasses of thickly sweetened tea. The carefree mixing of the sexes comes as a reminder that we are deep in Kurdistan, where—unlike much of the

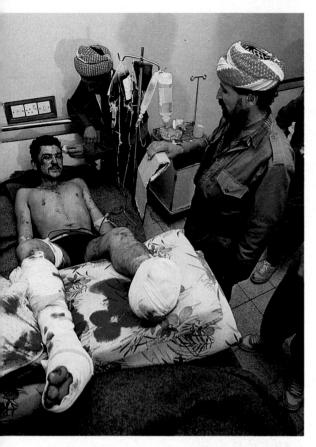

Middle East—women have traditionally not been secluded or veiled.

Fadime Kirmizi, a law student in her early 20s (page 52), comes in, accompanied by her brother. They find a table where the light is good and settle down with her law books. He quizzes her through the afternoon.

The afternoon's serenity is regularly broken by fighter jets screaming overhead, one after another, buzzing the city before returning to their Turkish Air Force base. To an outsider the jets seem a pointed reminder to the Kurds that they do not really belong. Yet to most of the Kurds I met, the attitude seemed to be expressed in the thought, what are the Turks doing in *their* country?

Dying of injuries from an Iraqi mine, a peshmerga lies surrounded by his comrades in the Zakhu hospital. In deserted Halabjah (below), a guerrilla inspects an unexploded bomb from a 1988 attack that killed some 6,000 villagers. A seven-year-old boy (opposite) was blinded by an Iraqi phosphorous bomb. He bears the scars of a generation too early acquainted with death and disfigurement.

TODAY'S KURDS find themselves caught between their ancient culture and the rush of the 20th century. At an embassy dinner in Turkey I was seated next to an Iranian woman. Her father was a banker, and she was married to an American, and when she heard of my interest in the Kurds, she exclaimed: "How fascinating! Of course, Khomeini treated them very badly, and they have resisted very bravely. But don't you find them really very—you know—*primitive?*"

In Shaqlawah, a beautiful but run-down town in northern Iraq that serves as a guerrilla headquarters for Free Kurdistan, I was witness to another demonstration of the same attitude.

It was early in June 1991, and the barren "negotiations" between Saddam and the Kurds were being conducted in the nearby town of Arbil. A handpicked Iraqi intelligence officer had been sent to Shaqlawah to escort rival leaders Talabani and Barzani to the meeting. Lieutenant Colonel Zeid, as he was called, arrived in an immaculate dark green uniform with carefully straightened black beret.

I was eyeing Lieutenant Colonel Zeid when a hoarse and raucous voice broke in. It belonged to a Kurd named Malazada, an unkempt local balladeer with a shell-shocked aspect. Impromptu, he stepped forward and began a long free verse recitation for the occasion. He went on and on, and the lieutenant colonel's clipped mustache began to writhe impatiently. Siamand Banaa, a public spokesman for Barzani's Kurdistan Democratic Party, touched my arm. "You'll have to excuse old Malazada," he whispered. "He's just missing a few strings, as we say."

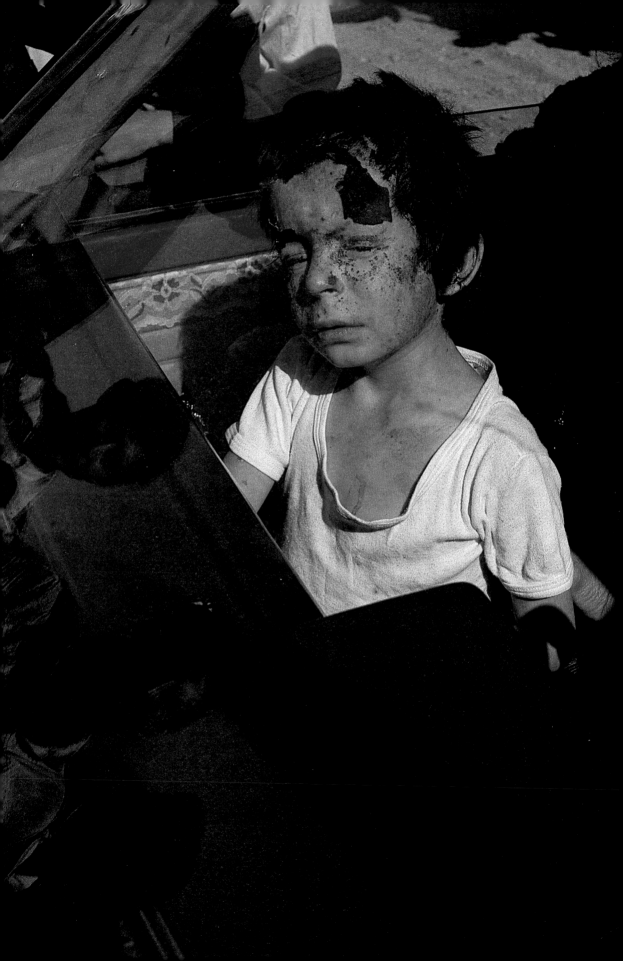

Rivals for power Masoud Barzani, at left, and Jalal Talabani battled each other to a draw on the May ballot for the position of paramount leader of Iraqi Kurdistan. Infighting has crippled Kurdish opposition to Saddam Hussein, and the winner of the runoff election will face formidable obstacles.

I appreciated the courtesy, but I rather liked the tolerance of the Kurds, who were willing to stall their big meeting for an old man whose liking for the village epic did no harm. In many ways I was miles and years away from his shaggy, verbose, bucolic style and his horizon bounded by tribe and the rhythms of seasons. The sight of the lieutenant colonel, who thought of these folk as barbarians, reminded me that many outwardly advanced types have taken little from development except technology, which they have employed for barbarous purposes.

ALL ACROSS IRAQI KURDISTAN you can drive for miles, map in hand, and mark off each succeeding heap of stones as the place where a village once stood. One by one the Iraqis dynamited or bombed or poisoned these communities in the name of repressing Kurdish insurgency and shifted their inhabitants into relocation centers. You can still see those too, bleak and menacing blockhouses, hemmed in with wire, where people who had known no master were confined and supervised. The Kurds have been hardened by the digging up of mass graves; estimates of the missing and dead range from 100,000 to 300,000. A United Nations report concluded that the atrocities committed by Saddam's regime were "so grave and . . . of such a massive nature that since the Second World War few parallels can be found." Yet in this landscape of blasted and deserted hamlets there are two sites that all the Kurds insist you must see: Qalat Dizah and Halabjah.

Qalat Dizah's turn came in June 1989. As a large market town near the Iranian border, it may have shown an independence of spirit that annoyed Iraqi military planners. They made an example of the place by bringing in the bulldozers and the dynamite. After the expulsion of the population—perhaps 70,000 individuals—the city was leveled house by house. Only the trees were left standing.

By the time I arrived, many of the former inhabitants, finding life insupportable in the refugee camps over the border, had returned to squat in the ruins of Qalat Dizah. A single tiny dispensary, run by a depressed doctor named Osman Salim, tried to hold the line against malaria, typhoid, and malnutrition. They were Osman's daily enemies, and he was combating them with almost zero resources.

"Exactly *nothing* has been done for the people of Qalat Dizah," he told me, complaining that the storied Western relief effort— which would eventually deploy millions of dollars in a hugely successful operation—had not yet trickled down here. The survivors faced another harsh winter, with unclean water and poor food and not nearly enough of either.

Not even this was enough to prepare me for the town of Halabjah, a community that has the same resonance for the Kurds as does the Warsaw Ghetto for the Jews or Guernica for the Basques. The town became suddenly and horribly famous on March 16, 1988, when it was almost obliterated by Iraqi bombs and its people were savaged by nerve gas and other poison agents.

"I saw the planes come," Amina Mohammed Amin told me through an interpreter. "I saw the bombs fall and explode. I tried to get out of town, but then I felt a sharp, burning sensation on my skin and in my eyes."

Mrs. Amin then did something that astounded me. Without warning, she drew up her voluminous dress and exposed her naked flank. Her whole left side, from mid-calf to armpit, was seared with lurid burns. And they were *still* burning.

"The Red Crescent took me to a hospital in Iran," she said, "and then I had five months in a London hospital. But the burns need to be treated every day." Even as we spoke, her daughters began applying salves to the exposed area. It was hard to look, and hard not to look.

Mrs. Amin said that 25 members of her family had been killed that day, which was a terrible figure even if you allowed mentally for the way Kurds talk of extended families. Nizar Hassan, the chief physician at the hospital, told me later that the town lost 5,000 people in the attack, out of a total population swollen by refugees to 70,000. (Later estimates pushed the doctor's body count above 6,000.)

I found one of the causes of the horror in a blitzed building. Here, lodged in a basement corner where it fell from an Iraqi Air Force bomber, was a wicked-looking piece of hardware with stencil markings on its side. Worried about fallout from the Halabjah escapade, the soldiers of Saddam had entered the town and carried off all the evidence. Or almost all of it. There was the bomb, and there were the survivors. Halabjah would, after all, be remembered.

46

Politics follow Kurdish immigrants from Turkey to Düsseldorf, where thousands march to protest the jailing of 16 Kurds belonging to a terrorist group that supports Kurdish independence. Khalil Barakat (below) fled to Cologne from Syria with his family of 12 in 1988 to escape political persecution. They are among an estimated 400,000 Kurds living in Germany.

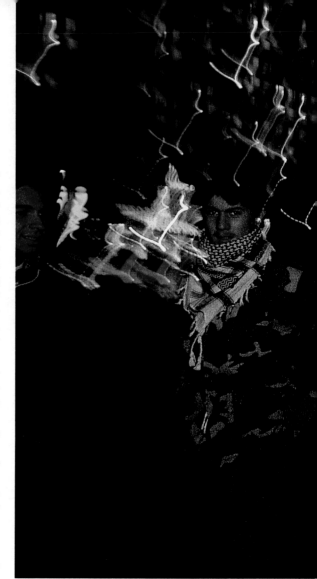

YOU CAN'T TAKE MUCH from people who have nothing to lose, yet I was impressed at how the Kurds make the best of hopeless situations. They are tough and adaptable, which is perhaps the key to their longevity in this war-ravaged region. Their resilience may face its latest test sometime this summer. Iraqi troops have been massing just outside Free Kurdistan, held at bay by fighter planes of the post-Desert Storm coalition. When that air cover is withdrawn, it is likely that the Kurds will again be under direct attack.

I was resting near the town of As Sulaymaniyah, then held by Iraqi troops. We were roasting a lamb for dinner. In every direction the land looked naked and lunar, stripped of life. It was hot. I wondered, out loud, if there was any beer in this wilderness.

"Beer," said one of my Kurdish bodyguards. "The Englishman wants beer!"

One of the fighting men dropped what he was doing and walked up to me. "How many Saddams you have?" he asked.

"Many Saddams," I replied.

We were talking money. Some of the bills in Iraqi currency are printed with the portrait of Saddam Hussein, leading the Kurds to joke incessantly about "dirty money."

"For 50 Saddams," the guerrilla said gravely, "I can bring quite a lot of beer."

I peeled off 60—it seemed no time for penny-pinching—and my man vanished into the dark. He was back in an hour, lugging an old sack containing cans of frosted Western ale.

"Ali, how on earth?"

Ali smiled, revealing nothing, but I suspected that he had struck a deal with a bored Iraqi guard in town.

A few days later, passing the war-scarred settlement of Rawanduz on our way back to the Turkish border, I saw other evidence of Kurdish enterprise. The owner of a roadside café had scrounged canned goods from somewhere and kept them chilled in a mountain stream, ready for sale. Small boys sold Western cigarettes still in their cellophane-wrapped packages. (How had they gotten them?) Families sat eating, half in and half out of cannibalized cars and trucks that were kept going on God knows what. The café proprietor and his wife were singing away, dishing up kabobs in exchange for fistfuls of Saddams.

These people had been bombed and routed, but they had come back and were evidently enjoying their moment of independence. Kurds, once regarded as suspicious of strangers, now took every Westerner as a friend.

"You will tell of us?" asked the old cook, as I pressed my last Saddams on him. "Tell people not to forget?"

The Kurds usually make their appearance in other peoples' narratives by virtue of a readiness to quit their mountain fastness and engage in battle. But their tendency is to go back to the mountains as soon as war is over.

Unfortunately, the Kurds live in an area that is strategically important to three great modern nationalisms, Turkish, Arabic, and Persian, and that is enormously rich in the two great natural resources of oil and water. The tendency of nationalism is to try to assimilate minorities and to invent a new "nation" such as Iraq (which is actually three communities, the Sunni Muslim ruling group, the southern Shiite Muslim majority, and the northern Kurds, mostly Sunni, rolled into one uneasy state). And the tendency of Middle Eastern politics is to establish control over oil fields and headwaters, not just for their own sake but before anyone else does.

The Kurds themselves have certain fundamental similarities. All are survivors. All are well acquainted with dispersal and persecution. But I began to discern variations in their

status throughout the region. In Jerusalem, for instance, there is a small but prosperous middle class of Jewish Kurds who live in peace. In Beirut, however, Kurds are the lowest of the low. A large Kurdish community has been in Lebanon since the beginning of this century, but on the identity card that Kurdish immigrants must carry, the words "domicile under review" appear in the space for citizenship. This puts the Kurds into a category of seasonal or migrant workers. In Lebanon the Kurd is almost always a menial, depicted by Lebanese novelist Elias Khoury as a faceless toiler and random victim.

Stateless in a state where statehood is itself a tenuous thing, Lebanese Kurds have thrown their support to the Kurdistan Workers Party, or PKK. This is a Marxist organization run by an enigmatic figure named Abdullah Öcalan,

Success in Turkey once exacted a heavy price—cultural assimilation. In Diyarbakır, the unofficial capital of Turkish Kurdistan, Kurds now vigorously pursue their rights in market and tea garden. Taking a study break, law student Fadime Kirmizi embodies the new opportunities opening up for Kurdish women.

HOSE IN THE RANK AND FILE of the PKK seem unaware that they are foot soldiers in the game of nations. Jawan and Soubhi, two young people who met me in Beirut, conducted me through a series of safe houses (never as reassuring as the phrase suggests, especially in Beirut). All my questions, they said, could be answered when I met the man they call Apo—Uncle: Abdullah Öcalan.

When I arrived at the camp known as the Mahsum Korkmaz Academy, for a PKK member who died in a battle in Turkey, I found hundreds of young people in well-cut, olive drab military fatigues, much more disciplined and military in aspect than any of the local militias, or indeed than either the Syrian or Lebanese Armies. Men and women mixed freely, a change from the monastic character of peshmerga camps in Iraq.

Hearing English spoken, I soon found myself talking with Milan, an olive-skinned teenager who had come from Australia, where her Kurdish parents had gone for work. Now she was a soldier in the war against Turkey.

"I'm trying to forget I ever knew English," she said. "All I care about now is Kurdistan." Unlike rival Kurdish parties in Iraq that seek autonomy within that nation, the PKK calls for a separate Kurdish state spanning the existing borders of Iraq, Syria, Turkey, and Iran. As if to prove her dedication, Milan had just been to a Maoist-style "self-criticism session," held under an awning just off the hot square at the camp's center. Face alight with belief, she invited me to watch rehearsals for the forthcoming PKK fiesta. In a few days tens of thousands of Kurds would converge on the camp for dances and speeches, with *Serouk Apo*—Apo the Leader—the guest of honor.

Apo himself, whom I met later that day, is a stern critic of the Kurdish people and their attachment to tradition. "We are a feudal society," he told me, "and our leaders have been chieftains who betray us. Our cultural and political level is low." He pointed to dark moments in the Kurdish past, such as the role played by Kurdish mercenaries in the Turkish slaughter of the Christian Armenians in 1915. He said that the Kurds were victims of the divide-and-rule mentality and could always be counted on to fight among themselves. There was some truth to all this, but Apo's own chieftain-like appearance and the tame eagle tethered rather eccentrically to his desk didn't inspire the absolute confidence he demanded.

with a camp in Lebanon's notorious Bekaa Valley. Here the PKK operates under Syrian protection, carrying on a guerrilla war against Turkey. Syria provides an umbrella for the same reason that umbrellas are always provided—water. In Turkish Kurdistan the huge new Atatürk Dam allows the Turks to control the flow of the Euphrates River before it crosses the Syrian frontier. Anxious for leverage, the Syrian regime uses the Kurds to remind the Turks not to exploit this advantage.

AN EXPERIENCED KURD can tell his grandchildren of betrayal by colonial Britain and France, of promises made by Iran, Iraq, Syria, and Turkey to support the Kurds for as long as they were fighting only on the rival's territory, of interventions in Kurdistan by Israel to weaken Arab nationalist regimes, and of promises made by both Cold War superpowers that turned out to be false.

Ever since President Woodrow Wilson incorporated promises for Kurdish autonomy into his Fourteen Points following World War I, the Kurds have traditionally looked to the United States as their deliverer from old injustices. George Bush appeared to sympathize with their cause during Desert Storm, yet his subsequent lack of support has left them baffled. Western politicians seem unable to appreciate the depth of the Kurdish yearning for a homeland. I sat with Jalal Talabani, leader of the Patriotic Union of Kurdistan, at his guerrilla headquarters in northern Iraq. He was telling me about the city he was most fiercely contesting with Saddam Hussein. "Kirkuk," he declared, "is our Jerusalem."

Lacking an alternative homeland of any kind, Kurds can emigrate, but they can't escape. In the grim factory belt that stretches between the Spandau and Charlottenburg areas of Berlin, Kurds work to produce the brand name goods of Osram, Siemens, and Volkswagen. The German government doesn't recognize them as Kurds but only as the Turkish passport holders that they are. They tend to cluster in rundown areas like Kreuzberg.

My guide to this world was a young man named Bayram Sherif Kaya, born in Germany of Kurdish parents who emigrated from southeastern Turkey. He divided his day between a Kurdish-language radio station, a kindergarten for Kurdish children, and various Kurdish relief organizations, all of which he helped run. "Fortunately I speak perfect German and I look European, so I don't have the problems that most of our people have."

Bayram doubts that he can go home again. "We are watched by the Turkish Embassy,

Embracing traditional ways, members of the Beritan tribe camp for the summer near Karlıova, Turkey. Despite government efforts to force them to settle down, these pastoralists migrate more than 500 miles round-trip between summer and winter pastures, subsisting on the milk, yogurt, and other sheep products they also sell in nearby markets.

Live ammunition focuses the minds of trainees at the Mahsum Korkmaz Academy in the Bekaa Valley of Lebanon. Graduates will join the PKK's insurgency in Turkey, where more than 3,700 people have been killed since 1984. Syria supports the PKK, using it as a bargaining chip in water-rights negotiations with Turkey.

which hates Kurdish nationalism. We are watched by Turkish extremists, who believe all Kurds are dogs. We are attacked by German fascists who shout '*Ausländer raus*—Foreigners out!' and paint it on our walls."

All over Kreuzberg, with its squatters and rent-controlled communes, were the slogans of different Turkish and Kurdish political factions. I paid a visit to Hînbûn, a women's center in Spandau that was originally founded to teach literacy but now serves as a sort of community center in hard times. "Most of the Kurds here come from one single town called Muş, in the Lake Van region of eastern Turkey," I was told by Aso Ağace, a Kurdish woman who works at the center. "Often they can speak German but not write it, so they need help with form filling, and they need help with the schools, which don't recognize Kurdish as a language."

Hînbûn is a counterpart to the male-dominated side of Kurdish life, in that it is for women only and acts as a support group. It tries to make Kurdish housewives and women workers feel more secure. "People are afraid," Aso Ağace told me. "We have also seen pressure from the Turkish Consulate on the municipal government of Berlin, which used to help us distribute our literature." Here, too, one found a sort of transplanted ghetto solidarity. The problem, as ever, was that of trying to survive as Kurds, while not seeming alien to a larger society.

I T IS DIFFICULT for an outsider to learn the essentials of the Kurdish cultural style. For one thing, although most Kurds who are Muslims adhere to the Sunni sect, some are Shiites; still other Kurds practice one of several indigenous religions. In addition, the Kurdish language is divided by dialects and subdialects. Kurds in northern Iraq, eastern Turkey, and the former Soviet Union speak Kurmanji, while those in western Turkey speak Zaza; in southern Iraq Sorani prevails, in Iran the Guran and Laki dialects. This problem of Babel is an impediment to Kurdish identity. Nonetheless, all Kurds can recognize Kurdish. Scholars at the Institut Kurde in Paris are at work on a Kurdish-French dictionary of about 50,000 words.

While this codification goes on, the mass of Kurds keep together with a sort of musical vernacular. During my sojourn in Iraq, for example, everyone was glued to cassette tapes

Commanding the devotion of tens of thousands of Kurds in Turkey, Syria, and Lebanon, PKK founder Abdullah Öcalan promises to lead them to the victory of an independent Kurdistan. Apo, or Uncle, as he is called, greets some of the 20,000 gathered at a festival in the Bekaa Valley to support the organization.

by singer Juwan Hajo, a Syrian Kurd whose productions are bootlegged all over the region. And in Diyarbakır the cassette business proved so popular that the Turkish authorities relaxed their ban on Kurdish music—the ban that my friend Hasan had so casually defied.

Kurds who have made the United States their home live in communities from California and Texas to Brooklyn, New York, where the Kurdish Library and Museum acts as a focal point for Kurdish affairs and crafts.

Most of them live in and around San Diego, where they began settling after the collapse of another Kurdish revolt in Iraq in 1975. The late Mustafa Barzani, father of political leader Masoud Barzani, came to the U. S. first, followed by a few hundred of his retinue.

A community leader sponsored a social evening for me in the suburb of Chula Vista. Though almost all present had made good lives for themselves, they struck me as stranded in time, compelled to watch the sufferings of their kinsmen from afar. They had all recently been, once more, taken up as a cause during the gulf war, and then dropped. There was much wistful talk, over tea and cakes, of the way it had been fashionable to be a Kurd during Desert Storm and of how newspapers never sent photographers any more.

"We are known as a refugee people," said Jamal Kasim, who runs a trucking business. He's a burly, smiling fellow who doubles as California spokesman for the Kurdistan Democratic Party. "So our image depends on the daily and weekly news," he went on. "People are generally friendly, and they sympathize with Kurds, especially since Halabjah, but Americans these days are not so interested in foreign affairs, and there are many who do not like immigrants of any kind."

Yet again, it seemed, the Kurds had pitched their tents in a difficult environment—the San Diego-Tijuana border, with its daily flux of illegals and its mounting anxiety over language, culture, and integration. (One local Kurd, I later found, had resolved the problem of his own assimilation by landing a job with the U. S. Border Patrol.)

Our gathering in Chula Vista included a food store manager, an architect, a free-lance journalist, and two computer engineers. Only one guest was unemployed. The two computer engineers worked for Ted Turner; one of them, Alan Zangana, was very proud of his company's having colorized "a film you may have seen called *Casablanca.*"

Successful as they were, though, I noticed again the absence of women, a tender subject that caused a mini-controversy when I brought it up. Alan Zangana picked up an argument I had been hearing off and on since I had innocently asked, back in Shaqlawah, where all the women had got to. One of my Kurdish guides then took to pointing every time he saw a female, as if to vindicate the good name of Kurdistan, "Look. There is one. Now

In and out of Turkish jails for political activities, 98-year-old Kurdish cleric Mele Abdurrahman lamented that he would not live to see a free Kurdistan; he died last February. Whether seeking autonomy or true independence, Kurds struggle to secure their place as a free people in command of their own destiny.

are you satisfied?" It is easy for Westerners to mistake the Kurds for backward fundamentalists, but Alan maintained that it was high time that women played an equal role in the political struggle. Nobody exactly disagreed, although I had the sense that I had stumbled into an argument they would have again.

I HAD ALMOST ABANDONED MY DREAM of finding a "typical Kurd" when I was introduced to Sheikh Talib Berzinji of Los Angeles. "Sheikh" is an honorific title; in the old country his family claimed descent from the Prophet Muhammad. Talib himself, with his leonine head and ample military mustache, is from the area of As Sulaymaniyah. He had been a follower of Mustafa Barzani— "Ah, the old general!"

He now divides his time between running a laundry service in Los Angeles, which he must do to make a living, and writing and translating plays, which he would do full-time if he could. He has translated *The Merchant of Venice* into Kurdish.

But his days are filled with the endless responsibilities of being a Kurd. The old sheikh explains to journalists and radio interviewers who the Kurds are and how long they have been fighting. He has to raise money for refugees. He has to think of his extended family back in the perilous mountains. A spread of the hands: "You see how it is."

If I had started my quest by talking to Sheikh Berzinji, a lot of what he said would have seemed either mysterious or self-pitying. But now I saw the stages through which he had passed. The Kurds are homeless even at home, and stateless abroad. Their ancient woes are locked inside an obscure language. They have powerful, impatient enemies and a few rather easily bored friends. Their traditional society is considered a nuisance at worst and a curiosity at best. For them the act of survival, even identity itself, is a kind of victory. The old man, holding on to his Kurdishness in a choice of hostile or indifferent environments, is the Kurd for all seasons. ☐

Denali

ALASKA'S WILD HEART

A bull moose ripples Wonder Lake beneath 20,320-foot Mount McKinley. Rich in wildlife, Denali National Park and Preserve has been called the Serengeti of the North, beckoning the hardy visitor.

By DOUGLAS H. CHADWICK

Photographs by DANNY LEHMAN

Sky opens wide for climbers on Mount McKinley, known to Indians as Denali, the High One. At 16,200 feet a snow wall serves as a windbreak. McKinley's summit, first reached in 1913, is now trod by some 500 people yearly.

T HIS ALASKA RIVER we're crossing pours out of a nearby glacier and braids its way down a gravel floodplain nearly a mile wide. The water is rock stew, so thick and gray you can't tell whether your next step is going to be a few inches deep or a few feet. Bet on a few feet. The flow is very high just now, swollen from several days of unusually hot June weather, and very strong. When you lift your leg, the current tries to toss it downstream; when you don't, the current eats away the gravel you're standing on and you sink by degrees. Larger rocks roll against your legs in the meantime, threatening to bowl you down. Their tumbling makes the whole river growl.

My companion and I grip a driftwood pole between us to steady each other's steps, and we keep our eyes fixed on the far bank so we won't be thrown off balance by the hypnotic rush of solid-looking surface. We make it through several channels but get into trouble on the widest one. We're fighting waist-high current. It's too late to turn around without spilling. The cold is deadening my legs when I need them most. Suddenly we're gone, swept loose. For a moment, as my heavy backpack drags me backward and under, I wonder if this ice water will grind my bones into more mineral grit. We thrash our way to a steep bank and cling to it for what seems a long time, too chilled and exhausted to haul ourselves out.

A couple of days, more river crossings, and a traverse of a steep slope of loose boulders later, we near McGonagall Pass, 5,720 feet above sea level (map, page 69). There we find a man sitting in the sunshine by a clump of dwarf willow. His lips are cracked and bleeding. Frostbite has left scabbed circles on his cheeks. But his eyes hold a rare brightness, and those hurt lips form a serene smile. It is as if he has just come from some realm of adventure that makes ours seem slight. In fact, he has. It rises above him and his coils of climbing rope.

Human iceman, David Kenison wears a leather nose guard while ascending the popular West Buttress route on Mt. McKinley, North America's highest peak.

Many begin their expedition on a glacier, arriving by ski plane such as one passing the mile-high east face of Mount Dickey (opposite), scaled by only a few expert climbers.

Look: There is a mountain so huge it seems to gather most of the light in the sky when the weather is fair and most of the clouds whenever storms arrive. And sometimes if you search above the topmost clouds, you find it still there, filling a part of the atmosphere where you would never suspect solid ground could be. A prospector named the peak after William McKinley, who was running for President at the time. Athapaskan Indians knew it by a more apt name: Denali—the High One. At 20,320 feet, nothing higher exists in North America.

The Alaska Range arcs some 600 miles from the Wrangell Mountains toward the Aleutian Range. In passing through the southern center of the state, it produces Mount McKinley and what the Indians call Denali's Wife—17,400-foot Mount Foraker—as well as 14,573-foot Mount Hunter

DOUGLAS H. CHADWICK writes often about wild creatures and places. He has completed a book on elephants, a subject he reported on in the May 1991 NATIONAL GEOGRAPHIC. Photographer DANNY LEHMAN's most recent GEOGRAPHIC assignment was "Mexico's Bajío—The Heartland," in December 1990.

and an outburst of other formidable spires. This section of the range in turn forms the backbone of Denali National Park and Preserve. At six million acres—slightly larger than the state of Massachusetts—it is the fourth largest unit within the National Park System. It is also the most accessible of all Alaska's large protected areas. And the most popular, for amid its overwhelming scenery, visitors can usually see more different kinds of large animals more easily than elsewhere.

Throughout, I find myself crossing invisible thresholds. They are the emotional equivalent of the firn line on a glacier, where snow turns into moving blue ice, or of the shift from evening light to alpenglow. They are where adventures become revelations.

In some nameless canyon during a pelting rain I step around a rock outcropping and find a wolf slowing down to stop and stare at me. Its gaze is frank, golden, lingering. Finally, it lopes on at the same unhurried pace as before.

DENALI
The High One

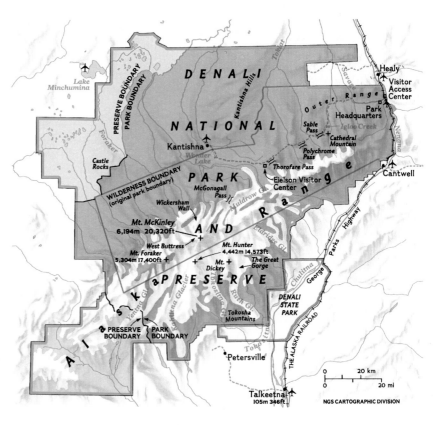

Icy upheaval captured by a satellite image (left), the Alaska Range includes Mount McKinley and its towering neighbors. Yet the park was created in 1917 not for its mountains but to preserve the largest of its 37 mammal species—grizzlies, caribou, Dall sheep, and wolves. In 1980 land additions tripled Denali to six million acres; snowmobiling, trapping, and other activities are permitted in the new areas. A single road runs through the heart of the park, and visitors must ride shuttle buses: Private vehicles are banned almost the entire year.

U. S. GEOLOGICAL SURVEY

I am left remembering the way water beaded around those eyes, wondering why I feel that words were somehow exchanged.

Farther on, in the Kantishna Hills, I meet Gary Laursen, a botanist from the University of Alaska. He names some of the miniature stars, bells, trumpets, and plumes that color the tundra all around us: Lapland rosebay, bearberry, alpine azalea, bog rosemary. . . . These wildflowers seem all the tinier in the shadow of Mount McKinley, and yet the

adventure Gary pursues begins beneath their petals. "Biologists once cut a sample core about the width of a nickel down into some tundra and picked out 16 different species of moss," he says. "The diversity underfoot can be like a tropical rain forest a few inches tall."

Helping us understand how nature really works is precisely the sort of thing Denali is supposed to do—a purpose underscored by its selection as a UN International Biosphere Reserve. At the same time, Denali is supposed

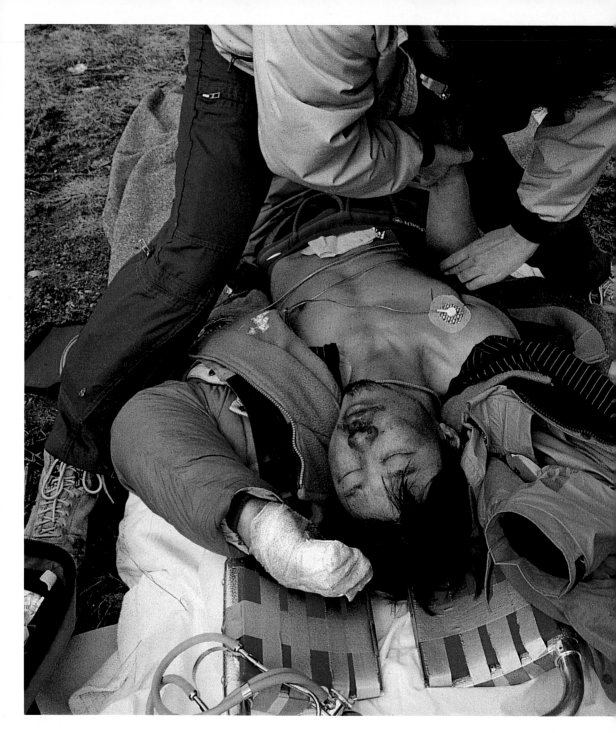

to provide recreation for visitors—serve as "pleasuring grounds for the public," to use a phrase from the early days of our National Park System. Mount McKinley National Park was established the year after the Park Service, in 1917; in 1980 it was renamed Denali National Park and Preserve. Fewer than 6,000 people came to the park in 1950. In 1990, 546,693. Visitors have more than doubled in the past decade alone, bringing up the question increasingly asked of parks: How many visitors can go a-pleasuring before the special untamed qualities get crowded out?

While new hotels, restaurants, gift shops, and subdivisions spread rapidly near the main entrance, just outside the eastern boundary, Denali's managers have been fielding proposals for more access routes and services within the still largely undeveloped park itself. Alaska politicians urge them to promote the sort of

BRIAN OKONEK

Hands frozen and face bloodied by a fall, Korean climber Beom Kyou Lee, rescued by helicopter on McKinley last year, awaits evacuation from Talkeetna Airport to Anchorage. He, an injured friend, and seven companions were lucky—they survived, unlike 70 others the mountain has claimed. A squad of Germans (above) are among the climbers who nevertheless attack the peak en masse. Japanese and British adventurers who made it raise glasses in Talkeetna's Fairview Inn.

high-volume, convenience-oriented tourism typical of, say, Grand Canyon or Great Smoky Mountains, hoping for tourism to help replace waning revenues from North Slope oil.

So now the question becomes: How much should a park be changed to suit people's needs and expectations? How much, bearing in mind that one goal of parks has always been to safeguard places *not* shaped by human demands. Places where we can go splash the spirit with pure natural wonder and freshen up the soul. Places that change us instead.

"We're facing choices many parks in the lower 48 faced 50 years ago," Superintendent Russ Berry says. "We still have one of the best chances to do it right." The decisions made today will influence the course of Alaska's less well-known parks and reverberate through those in the other 49 states. Our National Park System has been called the best idea the U. S.

ever had, and in some respects it surely is. Yet as Denali makes clear, the U. S. has never decided just what it wants its parks to be.

IN THE MIND of Denali's founder, naturalist Charles Sheldon, the area would serve mainly as a sanctuary for the outstanding big-game herds he observed between 1906 and 1908. Hunters were selling the wild meat to mining boomtowns. He foresaw worse carnage once the proposed Fairbanks-Anchorage railroad line speeded up transportation. Wealthy and well-connected, Sheldon persuaded Congress to safeguard more than 1.5 million acres between the top of the Alaska Range and a secondary fold of mountains to the north known as the Outer Range.

Almost every ridgeline below the realm of permanent snow is striped with wildlife trails. During May the caribou's ancient paths take them up mountainsides to share the Dall sheep's steep, rocky terrain, where they give birth to their calves. The migration is probably to avoid predators, but the caribou also find nutritious new sprouts at the edge of retreating snows and strong breezes that keep down the swarms of emerging insects. Usually. As I lay sweltering on a ridgetop, exhausted from following caribou tracks almost straight up and down talus slopes, I looked through the haze of biting flies and mosquitoes at a pile of boulder rubble in the center of a snowfield. Then a few boulders got up and shifted around to get more comfortable. They were caribou—nearly 50—taking refuge from the bugs amid the cool, white crystals.

In 1922 Mount McKinley National Park was expanded eastward to the Nenana River to take in a segment of railroad line and provide a site for the park headquarters. Wonder Lake, to the west, was added in 1932. A dirt road from the railroad depot finally reached that lake in 1937. Tourists could now motor almost 90 miles along the northern side of the Alaska Range. Of course, they had to bring their automobile in by railroad car, there being no other road anywhere close.

If you go due west from Denali, the nearest major highway you'll find is still somewhere near St. Petersburg, half the world away. However, a paved, all-season highway linking Fairbanks and Anchorage was finally completed in 1972, passing along the eastern side of the park. Visitation immediately doubled. Looking southward at examples such as

Yosemite, Denali's managers took several far-reaching steps to fend off the conflicts that can come with crowding.

In the Visitor Access Center near the park entrance, ranger Deb Greene tells me, "Not many people understand how we operate. They expect me to recommend which trail to take and where to camp, like rangers do in the lower 48." But this backcountry has no system of maintained trails. No designated campsites. No signs. No markers for river crossings. You have to take Denali on its own terms, the way the first adventurers found it.

Perhaps Denali's boldest move was to set up public transportation for the road to Wonder Lake, still the only route into the heart of the park, and ban private vehicles. Anyone can drive the first 15 miles to Savage River. Beyond that, forget America's love affair with the automobile; in Denali, you get on the shuttle bus. You can get off anywhere you please— as long as it's at least half a mile from a road sighting of wildlife.

Excuse me, driver, I'd like to step out here. The bus pulls away, you walk over a rise, and WHAM! It's just you and a few thousand square miles of true wilderness, the way it was before there was anything else in the world. Just you and the powerful heart of Alaska, with a line of caribou appearing over the next rise. And this bull moose shrugging its way through an alder thicket close by. And then miles of strolling across spongy tundra and along river bars, pausing to inspect the work of grizzly bears; they've cratered large stretches of gravel to get at the starchy roots of *Hedysarum,* a purple vetch sometimes called Indian potato. And then dark bodies in the willow brush . . . more moose: mother and calf, frequent testers of the wind, maybe a little unsure of what to do about your scent. You give them plenty of leeway, circle back to intersect the river, and end up quietly watching a pair of harlequin ducks feed in the riffles.

When you're ready to return to this century, you just flag down the first passing bus.

Or you can sit tight the whole time, look, and listen to a driver narrate the natural and human history of the park. I learn about James Wickersham, a judge from Fairbanks who led the first recorded attempt to conquer the High One. Approaching from the north in 1903, his party reached the base of an icy face now known as the Wickersham Wall. It rises sheer, without a major break for 14,000 feet.

*One last hardship—a cloud of mosquitoes—awaits climbers down from McKinley
after a successful month-long traverse, ascending one face and descending another;
the sleds on their backs hauled gear over snow. Biting insects also plague wildlife.
A caribou may lose a quart of blood a week to the ravenous swarms.*

Wickersham went a ways up one spur and, being judicious, said the hell with it. Heading back through the Kantishna Hills just north of Wonder Lake, he stopped to pan a few creeks for gold. The judge came up with enough color that he filed claims as soon as he returned. By 1905 gold seekers were stampeding to Kantishna. By 1906 the rush was already over. Charles Sheldon said that the only person who he was certain had made money was a lady of the evening. Nevertheless, prospectors have continued to work the hills off and on to the present day.

Before the next attempt on Denali can be told, the bus arrives at the Eielson Visitor Center, 66 miles west of headquarters. On this narrow, dusty road, that's maybe four hours of travel—given all the stops to view wildlife.

Eielson juts from a steep hillside to look out on a tremendous gravel plain of braiding river water and light, the Thorofare Pass. To the west rises the terminus of the 39-mile-long Muldrow Glacier, where green willows and poplar trees sprout from the debris atop giant ripples of ice. And beyond and above and creating all the rest: the colossal geometries of the High One. As a ranger prepares to lead people on a "discovery hike," a red fox sleeps curled up next to the steps, and a band of bull caribou strolls through the parking lot, hoofs clicking like the camera shutters on all sides.

"The caribou know me. I talk to them out the window of my room every day," says maintenance man Dave Minich, Eielson's sole human resident after the last bus pulls away each evening. "Heck, just 15 minutes sitting on the porch by myself, watching the fog rise or the morning sun paint the hills, and I feel like I'm talking to God."

On the way back our bus stops so we can view a grizzly with three cubs at Sable Pass, an area closed to hiking to give first rights to the many bears that frequent it. This family is grazing grass and a tall, white-flowered herb named *Boykinia* in a meadow freshened by snowmelt. The cubs are plain brown. Mom

has a classic Toklat coat—gold body with silver frosting, brown legs with a reddish tinge. As she sits, a cub races over to stand with its back against her, the better to wrestle the cub chasing it. Cub number three leaps into the air to bite at its mother's nose, and she gently swings her huge head to butt it away.

I am walking near the road by Igloo Creek not far from Sable Pass when a bus stops on the opposite shoulder. While passengers rush to peer out the far windows, the man at the wheel gives me a hand sign. I've learned most of the Denali drivers' code; a hand held antler-like and touching the brow means caribou, for instance. But what is a hand with fast-wriggling fingers plus a buck-toothed grin? I shrug. The driver waves me on board, then points to a little pika harvesting grasses in a rock pile.

LIFE DIDN'T SEEM SO LUSH in March when park naturalist Melanie Heacox and I joined rangers Al Smith and Gary Koy at the Wonder Lake ranger station. A storm added three feet of new crystals to a snowpack already deeper than usual. Winds shuttered the cabin windows with drifts and made icicles grow sideways from the eaves. We set out on a routine run with three dogsleds toward headquarters. Alone among our national parks, Denali is still regularly patrolled by dog teams.

Under good conditions the 85-mile trip might have taken no more than three days. Snowshoeing out a trail for the dogs and wrestling sleds in bottomless powder, it took us the better part of two weeks. Perfect. None of us were in any hurry to leave this wild bunch of country. White Dall sheep watched us pass below their wind-scraped cliffs. Whiter yet were the ptarmigan that whirred by like animated chunks of snow. At night there was singing; whether from our dogs or from wolves, I couldn't always tell. Each day brought new rhythms of pulling while mountains slid slowly and endlessly by.

In early April I continued to the southern, or coastal, side of the Alaska Range. It has milder temperatures than the northern, interior slope, but even deeper snow. A plane on skis dropped me near the upper end of 40-mile-long Ruth Glacier, one of 17 rivers of ice flowing off the slopes of the High One. I put on skis, clipped on to a rope between mountain guides Diane and Brian Okonek, and started to glide. Soon we were passing through the Great Gorge, where the Ruth has sliced an upraised granite mass into one of the most spectacular collections of walls on the planet. It's like the Grand Canyon without ledges. One exposure, the east face of Mount Dickey, soars 5,000 sheer, seamless feet. Make that 7,700; recent

sonar measurements reveal the glacial ice is at least 2,700 feet thick.

For a while I saw almost too much to absorb. Then the Ruth took a sharp bend and fractured into wall-to-wall crevasse fields. Just as we reached them, clouds that had been lowering from the summit settled onto us and began to leak snow. I found myself teetering on skis across thin ribs of ice, backpack tipping me one way, the sled that I hauled dragging me another, and all I could see now were the blue holes yawning on either side. The next day, snow-filled fog would completely erase what remained of the border between air and ground. My companions seemed to be floating

in luminous space at the end of their rope tethers. We couldn't tell a drop-off until our skis stuck out over the edge, sometimes not even then. In seven hours of trudging up, down, and around crevasses while avalanches poured off nearby cliffs, we covered no more than a mile and a half in straight-line distance.

The whiteout went on for days, until I felt I was living in a crystal labyrinth full of trap doors. Diane just shrugged, sending little cascades of snow off her shoulders, and said, "This isn't really bad weather for here. It's just weather."

On the morning that we finally worked our way off the side of the Ruth to cross the

Tokosha Mountains, the skies changed and the world came back. It sparkled and dazzled. It had distinct edges. More miraculous still, living things grew from it: the black bear that watched us drop down into the foothills, for instance. In short order we had stripped to T-shirts and were carving turns between thickets of alder and birch where butterflies—butterflies!—probed trickles of rising sap. Pairs of trumpeter swans were arriving to claim the earliest open water in the Tokositna Valley for nesting territories. It would be weeks before actual green-up, but I felt springtime more keenly than I had in years.

I was also beginning to feel how enormous and varied Denali is. The ranger station for the southern portion lies outside the park in Talkeetna. Although few hike into this rugged side of Denali, Talkeetna's flying services handle an increasing number of sightseers. The majority of McKinley climbers fly to base camps from here as well; the sleepy, winterbound village thaws to become a hive of slightly wild-eyed, summit-struck folk spouting foreign languages.

After climbing McKinley in 1942, cartographer Bradford Washburn led a 1947 expedition in which his wife, Barbara, became the first woman atop the summit. Not long after,

Fattening up on blueberries in September, a grizzly enjoys peace and quiet—for the moment. For four hectic days during that month, a total of 1,200 cars chosen by lottery are allowed on the park road. A close encounter with one of Denali's 200 grizzlies is perilous for foolhardy visitors (above).

Imposing granite monolith known as the Gargoyle rises 1,500 feet above

a trio of cross-country skiers on Ruth Glacier in the Great Gorge.

he began a National Geographic Society-sponsored project to create the most comprehensive map yet made of the peak. Working from airplanes, he noticed a possible new path to the summit. "It looked like the simplest, safest, fastest way, but it wasn't evident from below," Brad tells me. In 1951 he pioneered what became known as the West Buttress route, now followed by three of every four climbers. These days between 900 and 1,000 try for the summit each climbing season, from April until early July. About half make it.

Before adventurers take off to meet the High One, they must check in for a talk on safety with Denali rangers, overseen until recently by Bob Seibert.

"Our situation is different from almost anywhere," he explains. "We're only 350 feet above sea level, and though the top of McKinley is only 60 miles away, it's 20,000 feet higher. No matter how fit, no rescuer can race out of here and function at those extreme elevations without getting in trouble."

So Denali's climbing rangers patrol from a camp at 14,000 feet. Most mountaineers on the main route encounter them at least once. "We can clip a little device onto a finger and in 15 seconds measure oxygen saturation in the blood, a good indicator of how someone is adapting to the altitude," Bob continues. "Use of McKinley by climbers has been soaring, but the number who have had to be rescued has been going down."

I T IS GENERALLY SAID that as a result of additions made under the Alaska National Interest Lands Conservation Act (ANILCA) of 1980, the original park tripled in size from 2.2 million acres to 6 million. That is not exactly true. The amount actually added was almost 2.5 million acres, and it is a different kind of parkland than many people are familiar with: ANILCA provisions intended to preserve customary ways of life—permitting recreational snowmobiling as well as subsistence hunting, trapping, and fishing. And all those—plus sport hunting and unrestricted landing of airplanes—are allowed in two new areas adjacent to the park, totaling 1.3 million acres, added in the category of national preserve.

Ironies abound in such a hybrid system. Should a ranger catch you throwing granola to a friendly gray jay in the park, you might be chided for upsetting nature's balance. Yet you could hop on a snowmobile to go hunt grizzlies in the preserve. About 300 local residents, many nonnatives, qualify as subsistence users, entitled to hunt and trap within the park.

Under the terms of a 1971 act to settle land claims, Native Americans received "selected" federal land, about 60,000 acres of which became part of Denali under ANILCA. Such acquisitions have posed a serious concern for some Alaska parks, wildlife refuges, and other preserves. In a few instances owners have sold land, not to the government but to real estate speculators and developers. At the moment Denali managers don't foresee that the park will lose land—and anyway they have a different kind of headache, notably in the Kantishna Hills, where parkland annexed in 1980 came complete with active mining claims.

Recreational gold panning is perfectly legal in Denali. Since a 1985 lawsuit by the Sierra Club, however, commercial miners in all national parks in Alaska have had to submit a plan for meeting environmental standards. Few plans in Denali have much chance of approval. Past mining of heavy metals such as arsenic and lead has contaminated some Kantishna creeks. A better prospect for miners may be to sell their claims to the Park Service.

More than 500 acres of patented claims in the Kantishna Hills remain in private hands. Thousands more acres of unpatented claims could yet be "proved up," becoming private land. All of these, like native claim lands, could be sold one day. Right now, though, the pace of commercialization is limited because access is. Nevertheless, the state of Alaska intends to build a new road—open to private vehicles—to Kantishna, passing through northern portions of Denali. It could make Kantishna a center for hotels and services.

In its present form the park road offers an unparalleled North American wildlife safari experience. Yet because of limits on the number of vehicles, finding space on a shuttle bus at Denali's main entrance may require waiting a day or two during the peak of the season. The future will surely bring more visitors than ever. What to do?

Among the suggested solutions that won't increase traffic: double-deck buses and a more efficient reservation process. "But these are stopgap measures," notes Superintendent Russ Berry. "Sooner or later, we are going to have to think about saying, 'Sorry, the theater is full.' "

Love turned the world upside down for Nenita and Paul Farmer. The Filipina woman met Paul, a homesteader near Denali, in the lower 48 and moved to the far north to marry him. "She wears so many clothes in winter that she feels like an astronaut," Paul says, "but last January we had our honeymoon in Hawaii."

Pressures to allow more people, cars, and commercial enterprises into Denali come even as Yosemite tries to reduce general services within the park and Yellowstone is exploring a modern transportation system to reduce traffic congestion. Denali, hoping at least to offer visitors an alternative to the park road corridor—a different theater, so to speak—is studying ways to encourage use of its south side. These include trails and perhaps mountain huts in a few areas. Also, a major visitor center, possibly in Talkeetna or nearby Denali State Park, adjoining the national park. The 324,240-acre state park offers a fine trail system with abundant wildlife and spectacular views of the Alaska Range.

"We shouldn't force Denali to be all things to all people," I hear from Joe Van Horn, a member of a local conservation group called the Denali Citizen's Council. "Put the new tourist facilities and more developed forms of recreation on lands that are already managed for these uses, and let Denali be one place where we experience nature straight on. That's what I always expected of our wilderness parks but never found until I came here."

A FEW PEOPLE have told me that wolf researcher Tom Meier is starting to look a little more like his subjects every day. Something to do with the gray eyes beneath unruly hair, I imagine, coupled with his uncanny ability to turn up faint animal sign. In July, Tom prowls ahead of me for miles through the Outer Range, searching for a sheep carcass he spied from an airplane back in February. The animal had just been killed by wolves—the East Fork pack, Denali's largest, with 24 animals. Now, six months later, we finally locate a few white hairs washed down a little streambed. We follow them back uphill. Tom studies the lay of the slopes. "Where would a wolf have taken a piece to gnaw?" he says, as much to the wind as to me, then trots unerringly to a point on a ridge with a good view of the landscape. And

A trapper's rugged life drew Dan Hytry and Jeff Lesniak from Wisconsin in 1987. Getting from their home base at Lake Minchumina to a cabin at Castle Rocks in Denali National Preserve is a two-day bone-jarring ride; it also tears up the snowmobile, Dan finds (right). The young men work a trapline started by old-timers in the early 1900s. They take mostly marten, which Dan skins. The furs are auctioned in Canada.

there he turns up enough sheep bone fragments to identify the animal as an adult ewe, adding to his file of hard-won data on the age and sex of the wolves' victims.

In this wilderness so little influenced by human designs, Tom and his colleagues John Burch and L. David Mech recognize a rare opportunity to put together a picture of how large predators and prey operate within a full natural community. "We can get at questions like: Does having sheep as prey in an area lower the wolves' hunting pressure on moose?" Tom explains. "We're also looking at the relationship between wolves and grizzlies—and coyotes and foxes. We want to know the value to visitors of having wolves around. At the same time we're trying to figure out

what effect human activities have on wolves."

Almost all of these subjects happen to relate to the controversial question of whether or not wolves should be reintroduced to the world's first national park, Yellowstone. An especially important finding (because some people assume wolves will continue to increase until they ravage prey populations) is that the main cause of death among wolves within Denali turns out to be . . . other wolves. Aggression between neighboring packs tends to limit how concentrated these predators become. "Our evidence suggests that wolves would be beneficial to the Yellowstone ecosystem," Tom states.

The work of these biologists is confirming the findings of Adolph Murie, who studied wolves in Denali from 1939 until 1942. He was the first to document in detail the fact that wolves prey mainly upon the infirm, the old, and the young. At a time when America was still waging full-scale poison and trapping wars against predators—even inside national parks—Murie calmly pointed out that wolves would actually benefit prey species over the long run by culling the weaker members.

O N CATHEDRAL MOUNTAIN I watch a band of lambs playing amid patches of white-petaled flowers called avens. The lambs take turns leaping off a ledge onto a snowbank; all but one, which limps behind. Then they press together in a huddle, butting still hornless heads. The slowpoke joins in as best it can but remains a step or two late, unable to put its full weight on one foreleg. Yet the youngster looks well-fed. Its coat is still sleek. I do not see this lamb as wolf food. But I do see wolves when I look at it— wolves, bears, eagles; winter storms; frost prying loose footholds of rock; avalanches and gravity pulling down the scree slopes; glaciers rasping away whole mountainsides. I see the forces that cut and shape beauty. At the same time I see the forces that hold it together— snowpatches dissolving into soft piles of windblown dirt; mats of nitrogen-fixing avens and alpine forget-me-nots reaching up the slopes, binding the soil and making more; the mother coming over to the lamb to fill it with warm milk, even as a summer snow squall coats the blossoms with ice.

HEYA, HIYA, HODEEYO, BEARS. NO SURPRISES, OK? I'm following a different park scientist now: Carol McIntyre, bashing

Magpies scavenge a Dall sheep killed by wolves on the Toklat River.

In Denali about 2,500 of these wild sheep graze alpine pastures.

through thick brush full of fresh grizz sign. Laden with climbing gear, she crosses this valley beyond Polychrome Pass, scrambles up loose talus to a point overlooking a cliff wall, then lets herself down until she is sitting in a nest beside ground squirrel skulls, ptarmigan feathers, half a hoary marmot, and two growing golden eagle chicks. Slowly, methodically, she weighs and measures each eaglet, then crimps a metal band on its leg for identification. The first submits quietly. The other refuses to yield and pecks at her hand until it draws blood.

Since 1987 Carol has located 112 golden eagle nests in the Denali area. "This is the largest breeding concentration yet recorded in Alaska," she says. "I suspect that may simply reflect the effort we've put into counting them here. We're also keeping track of some 20 gyrfalcon nests. The gyrfalcons don't build nests of their own. They depend on unused golden eagle nests. We've found our golden eagles feeding on everything from wolf-killed moose to marmots to other predatory birds like northern harriers, short-eared owls, and ravens."

Not all the nests Carol monitors are within the park. "To fully understand population trends for these birds, we have to know what's happening to lands around Denali," she observes. "For that matter, we need to know

about their wintering territories as well." One eagle wearing a leg band from Denali was found wintering in southeastern Colorado. In 1990 Carol fitted an eagle with a radio transmitter and tracked it as far south as central Idaho before the battery gave out.

Who would have expected that the surfbird seen wintering along South America's Pacific shores would be found nesting on Denali's alpine tundra among ledges tracked by Dall sheep? The arctic warblers I hear singing in the tall willow brush where I shout to warn bears will fly to the vanishing tropical forests of Southeast Asia for winter. DDT sprayed on fields in Central and South America may have more to do with the breeding success of merlin falcons in Denali than any local conditions do.

Denali is an enormous park, but its real boundaries are much, much larger. True conservation is thus going to require cooperation on a larger scale than we have ever envisioned.

IT ISN'T EASY to get used to the idea of this place being incomplete and vulnerable when it appears so powerfully big. Some rangers who have worked in Denali for years have never been near its far northwestern corner, the Lake Minchumina area. Here the park named for North America's tallest mountain is flat as a beaver's tail for mile upon mile and dappled with lakes beyond counting.

For weeks the tundra I walked on in Denali's highlands kept changing color until the whole land took on the fire of midnight sun through clouds, of the rainbows that so often march along the north side of the Alaska Range as storms pour over the top. Now all the leaves in the lowlands are turning as well. The taiga is gold as Toklat grizzlies, eagle heads, nuggets; red as cranberries, foxes, spawning salmon. This is as close as I have ever been to living in a dream.

Scores of trumpeter swans gather in Minchumina's bays, staging for their autumn flight south. Sandhill cranes from Siberia pass through trailing clarion calls, bound for the southern U. S. At one point more than 300 wheel upward over the lake like angels caught in a whirlwind, gaining altitude for their journey over the distant Alaska Range.

I'm headed that way myself soon. Despite all the discussions of problems I heard and all the proposals for improvements, Denali gave me everything one could hope for from a wild place. Then it gave me more than I knew how to hope for: new ways of seeing, feeling, and knowing that spring from direct contact with grand natural patterns. By way of honoring Denali in return, I would say I do not see how we can make this place any better. We can only seek the best ways to keep it as it is. □

PARAGUAY

In full dress for Independence Day, officers gather to parade through the capital city of Asunción. Long ruled

Plotting a New Course

By SANDRA DIBBLE <small>NATIONAL GEOGRAPHIC EDITORIAL STAFF</small>
Photographs by ALEX WEBB <small>MAGNUM</small>

by dictators, wary citizens wonder if shadows of military rule menace their flickering democracy.

Homeless after a military eviction in Alto Paraná, squatters huddle in a shelter. Land is plentiful in Paraguay, but reform has been slow, and thousands of peasants have staged peaceful occupations of large properties.

W EEPING and coughing, his longish brown hair and dark suit drenched, Asunción's new mayor stood helpless as tear-gas canisters flew and fire engines spewed jets of water along Calle Palma, the city's major shopping street.

On this warm spring day, bus drivers were striking in Paraguay's capital city. Protesters filled the street, shouting at hundreds of policemen drawing closer. But no one was taking orders from Carlos Filizzola, Asunción's first elected mayor in 454 years.

In Paraguay it's sometimes unclear who's even giving the orders these days. The country's transition from the longest dictatorship in 20th-century Latin America seems like a roller-coaster ride, with the passengers uncertain of the ups and downs ahead.

The ride began with a military coup in February 1989. After 35 years of running Paraguay like his private feudal estate, Gen. Alfredo Stroessner, 76, president of the republic and fierce anticommunist, was sent packing by his own right-hand man, Gen. Andrés Rodríguez.

To everyone's surprise Rodríguez freed the press, pushed for economic reform, and promised democracy. He then won a presidential election, plunging his 4.5 million countrymen down the uncertain track they call *La Transición*.

"An island surrounded by land" is how the Paraguayan novelist Augusto Roa Bastos described this California-size country. Landlocked and dwarfed by larger, more populous neighbors, Paraguay has been a backwater since colonial days. There was no gold to attract conquistadores, just thick forests, rolling hills, and friendly Guaraní Indians.

Politics reinforced the country's natural isolation. Between 1811 and 1840 the first dictator all but sealed its borders, and later, the War of the Triple Alliance against Argentina, Brazil, and Uruguay claimed the lives of nine-tenths of its adult male population. Then as now Paraguay's salvation lay in its fertile soil, and today it remains South America's most rural nation.

In October, when I arrived for a two-month visit, a sudden cold spell had scattered violet jacaranda blossoms over Asunción's broken sidewalks. A harp festival was under way, and for seven nights Asuncenos flocked to hear Paraguayan polkas and the languorous songs they call *guaranias*. On Calle Eligio Ayala waiters with bow ties and courtly manners served customers beneath the breeze of slow-moving ceiling fans. Off the Plaza Uruguaya a wood-burning locomotive chugged out of the 130-year-old railroad station and headed for Paraguay's southernmost city, Encarnación.

"Tranquilo," people would reply when I asked how they enjoyed their jobs, their neighborhoods, or simply how they happened to feel that day. But some weeks later, when police and tear gas filled Calle Palma, I saw that life could be other than tranquil.

Good times are a sure bet for a lunchtime crowd at the Asunción racetrack. In a wealthy neighborhood across town, jaguars Chaco and Luna eye Simón the schnauzer at a mansion they share with Manuel Battilana Peña; his other animals include 15,000 head of cattle.

A mirror reflects a market crowd in old Encarnación. Merchants there must move before a dam on the Paraná River floods their 19th-century neighborhood and 300 square miles of Paraguayan countryside.

At the foot of downtown Asunción more than 20,000 people share the shacks and dirt roads of the teeming barrio called La Chacarita. Proximity to stores, jobs, and transportation keeps residents in this hilly riverside shantytown.

When it seemed my throat and eyes had caught fire from the gas and I could no longer see my way past Calle Palma's 19th-century buildings, I felt a small hand slip into mine and pull me across the street. *"Vení, señora. Sentate, señora,"* a young woman's voice said. "Come, señora. Sit down, señora." She sat me on a stool and handed me a soft drink for my throat and some water for my eyes.

She was a sidewalk vendor named Ernestina Salinas, a petite woman of 24 with gentle motions and a sorrowful expression. She and her husband sold women's makeup from a table every morning near the corner of Calle 14 de Mayo. Business was slow, she said. Some days they were lucky to sell even an eyeliner pencil.

I would, in the weeks to come, find many Paraguayans who cushioned the uncertainties of their lives with the same natural civility and generosity that Ernestina had shown. Those who had the least usually gave the most: a bed, a seat on a crowded bus, a piece of freshly picked fruit, a sip from a communal gourd of the hot and bitter tea known as maté.

"This is still a place of innocence," an American acquaintance told me when I arrived. It wasn't just the setting of faded old buildings, brightly painted buses with wood floors and sputtering engines, dirt roads that snaked toward hamlets lost in the green countryside. Paraguayans themselves seemed to step from an earlier and simpler time.

NUESTRA SEÑORA Santa María de la Asunción— how sonorous was the full name of the capital. It was founded in 1537 by the Spanish explorer Juan de Salazar. It served briefly as the Spanish empire's capital in southeastern South America, then faded as Buenos Aires rose to prominence.

Asunción seems like a small town when compared with most of the other great Latin American capitals, yet in Paraguay it dominates, with 1.2 million people in its metropolitan area—more than a quarter of the nation's population. It is the transportation hub, the seat of the nation's five daily newspapers, and the undisputed center of political power.

Thus the election of Mayor Filizzola in May 1991 was a political landmark, almost rivaling the coup itself. "The law of *mbarete* is over," proclaimed one headline, using the

Paraguay

"Liquid spinal cord of my country," essayist Helio Vera wrote of the Paraguay River, which drains and separates this landlocked nation into distinct halves. Most people live in the fertile eastern region. Floods, drought, and high winds have kept most settlers away from the Chaco, a plain that takes up 60 percent of the country but is home to less than 2 percent of Paraguayans.

SOUTH AMERICA

AREA: 157,048 sq mi. **POPULATION:** 4,520,000. **RELIGION:** Roman Catholic. **LANGUAGES:** Spanish, Guaraní. **LIFE EXPECTANCY:** 67 years. **PER CAPITA INCOME:** $1,000. **ECONOMY:** Food products, forestry products, illegal trade. **EXPORTS:** Soybeans, cotton, beef, timber.

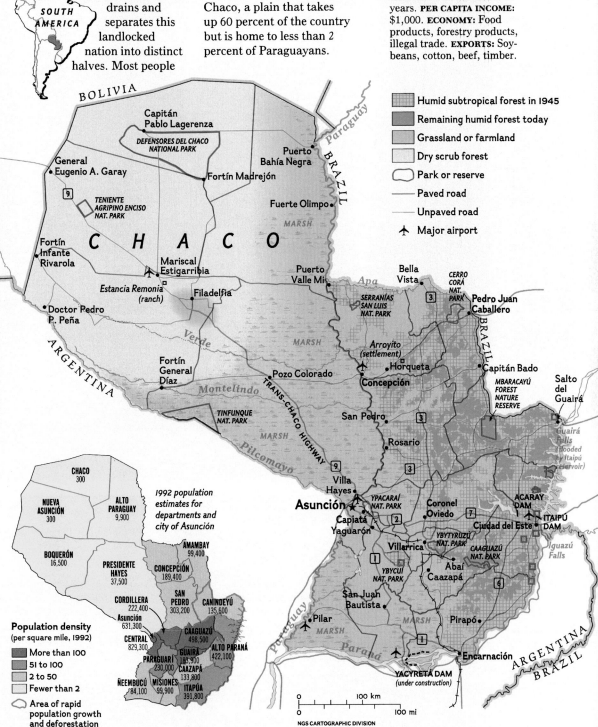

Humid subtropical forest in 1945
Remaining humid forest today
Grassland or farmland
Dry scrub forest
Park or reserve
Paved road
Unpaved road
Major airport

BOLIVIA

Capitán Pablo Lagerenza

DEFENSORES DEL CHACO NATIONAL PARK

General Eugenio A. Garay

Puerto Bahía Negra

Fortín Madrejón

TENIENTE AGRIPINO ENCISO NAT. PARK

Fuerte Olimpo

MARSH

C H A C O

Fortín Infante Rivarola

Mariscal Estigarribia

Puerto Valle Mi

Apa

Bella Vista

CERRO CORÁ NAT. PARK

Pedro Juan Caballero

Estancia Remonia (ranch)

Filadelfia

SERRANÍAS SAN LUIS NAT. PARK

Doctor Pedro P. Peña

ARGENTINA

Verde

MARSH

Arroyito (settlement)

Horqueta

Capitán Bado

MBARACAYÚ FOREST NATURE RESERVE

Salto del Guairá

Fortín General Díaz

Pozo Colorado

Concepción

Montelindo

TINFUNQUE NAT. PARK

San Pedro

Rosario

Guairá Falls (flooded by Itaipú reservoir)

Pilcomayo

MARSH

TRANS-CHACO HIGHWAY

9

Villa Hayes

Asunción

YPACARAÍ NAT. PARK

Coronel Oviedo

ACARAY DAM

ITAIPÚ DAM

Capiatá Yaguarón

2

Ciudad del Este

Iguazú Falls

Villarrica

YBYTYRUZÚ NAT. PARK

CAAGUAZÚ NAT. PARK

1

Abaí

YBYCUÍ NAT. PARK

Caazapá

San Juan Bautista

Pirapó

Pilar

MARSH

Paraná

Encarnación

ARGENTINA
BRAZIL

YACYRETÁ DAM (under construction)

BRAZIL

Population density map

1992 population estimates for departments and city of Asunción

CHACO 300
NUEVA ASUNCIÓN 300
ALTO PARAGUAY 9,900
BOQUERÓN 16,500
PRESIDENTE HAYES 37,500
AMAMBAY 99,400
CONCEPCIÓN 189,400
CORDILLERA 222,400
SAN PEDRO 303,200
CANINDEYÚ 135,600
Asunción 631,300
CENTRAL 829,300
CAAGUAZÚ 498,500
GUAIRÁ 183,900
ALTO PARANÁ 422,100
PARAGUARÍ 230,000
CAAZAPÁ 133,800
ÑEEMBUCÚ 84,100
MISIONES 99,900
ITAPÚA 391,800

Population density
(per square mile, 1992)

More than 100
51 to 100
2 to 50
Fewer than 2

Area of rapid population growth and deforestation

0   100 km
0   100 mi

NGS CARTOGRAPHIC DIVISION

Charred remnants of a once lush forest burned for cattle pasture mark old hunting grounds of Aché and Guaraní Indians in Canindeyú. Near undisturbed tribal lands in the eastern Chaco, Chamacoco Indians bathe in the Paraguay River.

bonuses last year, he was forced to seek private bank loans. "They've marginalized us," the mayor fumed.

If Filizzola appeared frustrated, Martin Burt seemed energized. "Things are changing so fast that politicians are lost—they don't know who to talk to," said Burt, 34, Paraguay's new under secretary of commerce. Burt came to government after Stroessner's overthrow and is working furiously to help move his country toward the future. "Many people are cynical because some things are not changing," he told me. "But there is transition—things will never be the same."

Asunción always seemed to be pulling in different directions, lunging forward and then suddenly withdrawing into old ways. The country's isolation under Stroessner was so long and so complete that even old ideas find new life in this slow-paced city. As communism crumbled around the world, members of Paraguay's tiny Communist Party convened openly for the first time. And beneath the tall trees of the Plaza Uruguaya an open-air bookstore prominently displayed works previously banned: volumes by Marx and Engels and a biography of Castro.

The lifting of repression has its price: Throughout the country street crime has risen. "Before, everything was more tranquilo," my 24-year-old hairdresser, Fátima Espinola, sighed as she blow-dried my hair in her narrow two-chair salon in downtown Asunción. But if people are unhappy, they can now at least say so.

THREE-QUARTERS of Paraguayans live outside the capital. Twelve hours and worlds away from Asunción, I was walking between dense forest and newly cleared land. I had left the capital by military plane at sunrise; in Concepción I switched to a bus that blared sentimental Paraguayan country music; then outside Horqueta I climbed on the back of a farmer's motorcycle for the final stretch. The bike's clutch soon broke, so the farmer and I continued on foot, our feet sinking with each new step into fine red sand.

At sundown we reached Arroyito. Lost in the wilds of central Paraguay, this small community was started by squatters and embodies the country's most sensitive political issue: the struggle for land by destitute peasants.

Guaraní word for strongman. The 31-year-old mayor was a physician and labor leader; he had been jailed repeatedly by Stroessner for organizing public-hospital workers. He was supported—against the entrenched Colorado and other parties—by a year-old coalition called Asunción para Todos—Asunción for All.

But winning office was just the beginning of Filizzola's political struggle. He was an outsider, and a mayor's power is limited. By law the central government controls the police, labor negotiations, and a large part of municipality budgets. It seemed nobody had to listen to him. To give underpaid employees

German-speaking Mennonite children—one with a BB gun—head for school in Filadelfia, founded by the pacifist religious sect in the sparsely populated central Chaco. A cultural crossroads, the area houses thousands of Indian laborers, whose children (below) play and study apart from their Mennonite neighbors.

In Arroyito I found several hundred families squeezed into hastily raised huts with thatched roofs and red dirt floors. Filthy babies wept and swatted flies. Two wells didn't supply enough water, so a government truck was bringing more every other day—still not enough. "The situation is repulsive," a young resident complained.

There is only one tractor and few oxen or plows, so farmers work their fields of cotton and manioc with hoes. Yet Arroyito marks a step upward for its inhabitants.

"Paraguay," the saying goes, "is a nation of men without land and land without men." There is plenty of land in Paraguay: With 29 people per square mile, it is one of the world's most sparsely populated countries. Since most of the property is controlled by only a few landowners, Paraguay's land distribution is among the most skewed on the continent.

The problem dates back to the War of the Triple Alliance from 1865 to 1870, which left Paraguay financially ruined. To raise money, the government sold off public lands to foreigners. For decades there was so much land and so few people that the question of property ownership lay dormant. But in the 1950s and '60s, with population growing and demand for cotton, soybeans, and other crops rising, the struggle for land began.

Dejesús Sosa, now a wiry man of 48, set out to address this problem a few years ago when he lived adjacent to what is now Arroyito. He then had nine acres and ten children. "We struggled, we struggled, but it made very little difference. We had no hope of rising from our poverty."

Sosa's promised land lay across the highway: 34 square miles of forests and prairies owned by the Unión Paraguaya livestock company. When he and his fellow farmers first asked for government help in obtaining the property, they saw no results.

On April 12, 1989, more than 1,200 people took over the land, joining thousands of frustrated peasants across the country who conducted similar peaceful invasions following the February coup. Though soldiers evicted Sosa's group within five days, Unión Paraguaya was eventually forced to sell the land to the government. The farmers were allowed back, with promises that they would be able to buy the property.

Obtaining land was just the first step for Sosa and the others. They now clamor for credit. "To give credit, the banks ask if we have oxen, cows, horses—if we have plows and property titles," said Sosa.

Despite the difficulties, the people of Arroyito seem hopeful, with ready smiles and easy manners. Most understand Spanish but prefer to use Guaraní. I soon learned to love the slow and lilting rhythms of their language, Paraguay's most commonly spoken tongue. "¿Mbaéichapa?—How's it going?"—they would greet me; they taught me to answer, "Iporante—Just fine."

The people of Arroyito are proud of their Paraguayan heritage, a blend of Spanish and Indian born in the 16th century when Spanish settlers took Indian wives. Today Paraguay is the only Latin American country where nearly everyone—from the president on down—speaks the same Indian language. The vast majority consider themselves mestizo, of mixed blood.

Soon after arriving in Arroyito, I befriended Dominga Mendoza, 20, one of three young women trained by the Roman Catholic Church to give basic medical assistance. When I asked to hear a Paraguayan polka, she belted out a tune, grinning as she sang like a country music star. We biked through the settlement, she guiding the thick rubber tires down uneven paths while I struggled to hang on. She brought me to her family's hut and prepared mbeju, a local favorite made of ground manioc patted into a cake and fried over a fire. It was a wonderful breakfast.

At night seven of us slept on three beds in a single room: Dominga; her sweet and shy cousin Agripina with her husband, Miguel Angel, and son, Edgar, ten; their chatty niece, Carolina, four; Edgar's friend Eusebio; and me. Inside the wood shack, human sounds pierced the early morning darkness: a snore, some whispers, a kiss. Outside, a rooster crowed, then another, and another.

NOWHERE is Paraguay changing as quickly—or visibly—as in the Itapúa and Alto Paraná regions bordering Argentina and Brazil. As I drove north from Encarnación on Ruta 6, charred tree trunks stood like broken survivors on the barren and smoking ground. Forests were being cleared for farmland, but it seemed more like the wreckage of some terrible battle.

The softly sloping lands along the Paraná River are Paraguay's richest, blessed with

Sips of bitter tereré tea cool off estancieros on a Chaco ranch. They are no pickup-truck cowboys says an admiring neighbor: "These men can handle a horse with the best of them."

regular rainfall and nutrient-rich soil. Jesuit missionaries in the early 17th century appreciated this and organized the Guaraní Indians in the area into self-sufficient agricultural communities known as *reducciones*. Three centuries later the Swiss naturalist Moisés S. Bertoni declared that the lands "reach a point of fertility that surely very few lands on earth can match, or perhaps they even are superior to all the others."

Bertoni would no longer recognize the hills he so lovingly described. In recent decades mechanized agriculture and the increasing world demand for soybeans have helped transform the sylvan landscape into a tidy patchwork of fields. Compounding the pressure on the forests are an estimated 400,000 Brazilians—farmers and their families fleeing rising land prices in their own country.

"The most admirable aspect of Paraguay," Bertoni wrote, is "its virgin forests." He would shudder today. Between 1945 and 1985 eastern Paraguay lost 12.4 million acres of forest. With the scramble for land that followed Stroessner's overthrow, the deforestation intensified.

"Other countries have modified their behavior, but not us," said César Berni, the young Australia-trained head of Paraguay's tiny forestry service. "We haven't become

being built with Argentina and is scheduled to come on line by 1995. By then Paraguay will be the world's largest exporter of hydroelectric energy—an ironic position for a country where four out of ten people don't even have a light bulb to turn on. But a hundred-million-dollar loan from the Inter-American Development Bank is helping Paraguay take electricity to the rural areas of the east.

I HEADED to Ciudad del Este, a city that did not exist 35 years ago. Today, with 150,000 inhabitants, it is Paraguay's fastest growing and second largest city, and its capital of contraband. Every day Brazilians cross the Friendship Bridge over the Paraná River to flood the business district. They fill bags with cameras, calculators, Scotch whisky, tapes, toys, watches, sunglasses, jeans—any foreign goods that the Brazilian government has effectively banned through high protective tariffs. Then they trudge back across the bridge to Brazil.

Contraband also flows the other way, from Brazil into Ciudad del Este: oranges, soft drinks, tanks of cooking gas, freshly killed chickens, plastic-foam coolers, bags of sugar and flour—anything that sells cheaper in Brazil than in Paraguay.

The frenzied trade is called *contrabando hormiga*—ant-size contraband—the hundreds of scurrying load bearers resembling ants. If the amounts are small enough, Paraguayan customs agents look the other way; a little bribe eases the way for bigger shipments. Everybody knows the rules.

Economists estimate that about 40 percent of Paraguay's trade is contraband, much of it passing through unregistered airstrips. "What the 'ants' carry is not the big problem," Fernando Masi, an economist, told me. "The big problem is the large operators who bring in four to five containers from

conscious of the gravity of the situation."

Changing the landscape too is the world's largest hydroelectric project, the 20-billion-dollar Itaipú Dam on the Paraná River between Paraguay and Brazil.

Begun in the mid-1970s and completed last year, Itaipú's 12,600-megawatt capacity is 20 percent larger than that of its closest competitor, Guri Dam in Venezuela. Itaipú's massive ramparts rise 60 stories; its reservoir stretches a hundred miles upstream, drowning Guairá Falls.

Paraguay uses less than 5 percent of the Itaipú Dam's energy, Brazil the remainder. Yacyretá, a smaller dam on the Paraná, is

Young athletes take a break between games at a nursery school in Pirapó, one of six farming communities founded by Japan, Paraguay's largest foreign-aid donor. Outside the Mbaracayú Forest Nature Reserve, an Aché youngster watches his elders raise a school in the rain forest.

abroad, take them by truck or plane to Ciudad del Este, then fly them out from secret airfields to Brazil."

Ciudad del Este's contraband is journalist Héctor Guerín's beat. Once a week his tiny portrait, young and defiant, stares from the regional pages of *ABC Color,* Paraguay's largest daily. "In Paraguay, as in all countries, there is corruption," he told me. "In Ciudad del Este, it's an everyday thing. All done in broad daylight. Nobody hides."

Stifled under Stroessner, Paraguay's press has emerged a powerful player, and Guerín is among those testing the limits of this new role. The coup has been a mixed blessing. Guerín now writes freely, and his newspaper, closed under Stroessner, will print what he writes. But there are risks: Guerín has been beaten and subjected to death threats because of his articles. Members of the local Colorado youth group marched against him, and a businessman he denounced sued him for defamation of character. "I want to leave this place," Guerín said, "but if I leave, I'll be a coward."

We cruised the business district in his white pickup, squeezing past rows of sidewalk merchants. "That was built by money laundering," Guerín would say, pointing to an office building, or "That's a front for the Cali drug cartel," nodding toward a busy department store.

Last year Guerín drew national attention with a series in *ABC Color* about the private airstrips outside Ciudad del Este that are used for smuggling. The government closed two airstrips, but Guerín is convinced the illegal trade continues. "The saddest thing," Guerín said, "is that one denounces and denounces, and nothing ever changes."

But sometimes it does. In March 1991 the Paraguayan government agreed to join Brazil, Argentina, and Uruguay in a South American common market known as Mercosur. The elimination of trade barriers between the four countries will have far-ranging consequences for all of Paraguay. But the effect will fall with most force here in Ciudad del Este.

"It is a city that could disappear when Mercosur is in place, since most of its business is contraband," Fernando Masi had told me. He is a founding member of IDIAL, a private institute promoting Paraguay's economic integration with other Latin nations.

THE TOLL TAKER at Pozo Colorado on the Trans-Chaco Highway stopped slapping himself just long enough to grab my thousand-guaraní note — about 75 cents. *"Muchos bichos,"* he muttered, "many bugs," and slammed his booth door. Night was falling, and I could barely see the road through the crush of insects that rapped the windshield like a soft, steady rain.

This was Paraguay's Chaco, one of South America's last frontiers. Some call it the "green hell"; others, the "drunken forest," for the bottle-shaped trunks of the spiney *samuú* trees that seem to step from some make-believe land. Paraguay sends its most brutal criminals here to a prison so remote that it needs no bars: Those who escape die of thirst.

The Chaco is Paraguay's Wild West. About 65,000 people — mostly cattle ranchers, Indians, Mennonites, and soldiers — share this huge semiarid plain separated from the rest of the country by the Paraguay River.

The temperature can reach 110°F every day for weeks. Some years it doesn't rain for months. Chaqueños will tell you how the wind blows, the groundwater is salty, the mosquitoes bite, the grass is bitter, the brush is filled with poisonous snakes. They'd never live anyplace else.

"You feel good in this place," said Franz Gunar Duerksen. "You fight with the climate, you fight with the land, and you get something for your fight. You don't get that in eastern Paraguay."

He was a tough, red-haired Chaqueño, tall and strong, with pale skin that freckled even beneath the brim of his cowboy hat. Just 22, he felt at home on the lonely rutted trails of Estancia Remonia, the cattle-breeding ranch he helps manage for German investors.

He is a Mennonite, born and raised 30 miles southeast of the ranch in the town of Filadelfia. About 22,000 Mennonites live in Paraguay in 20 settlements, the three oldest and largest in the central Chaco.

Mennonites are pacifists, a breakaway sect for whom the Reformation did not go far enough in separating church and state. They trace their origin to the early 16th century in Switzerland, the Netherlands, and Germany. Often persecuted, many moved in the 18th century to Ukraine and in the 19th century to Canada and the United States.

The first community in Paraguay was

"Buen precio—good price," murmur the street merchants of Ciudad del Este. The commerce of this border city runs on penny-ante contraband to satisfy bargain hunters from Brazil.

established in 1927 by a group from Canada. The second arrived in 1930 from Russia.

The Mennonites have their own language, a Low German dialect called Plattdeutsch. In the Chaco they maintain their own roads, phone system, and electric plants. They teach in their own schools, train their own nurses, pass their own budgets, pick their own juries, issue their own traffic tickets, run their own jail cells.

"If we waited for the Paraguayan government, poor things, we'd be dead," a Canada-trained Mennonite doctor explained as our footsteps rang through the spotless hallways of a new 75-bed hospital.

Only 12,000 Mennonites live in the Chaco, but their importance far outstrips their numbers: They produce roughly half of Paraguay's milk and most of its peanuts. On one of the earth's least inviting spots, the Mennonites have not only survived but thrived. Outside financial help from supporters in the United States, Germany, and elsewhere has been crucial, strong community ties even more so. "That's absent in Paraguayan culture. They just fight, fight, fight, and don't get any consensus up," said Jacob Harder, principal of Filadelfia's only high school, which is bilingual in Spanish and German.

After years of isolation in the central Chaco, the self-reliant Mennonites are feeling vulnerable. In Asunción legislators have begun denouncing the community as a "state within a state," and Indians under their domain are beginning to complain publicly.

My first morning in Filadelfia, a stiff wind carried a soft, white-brown Chaco dust, giving the town a muffled feel. I passed some Indians along Avenida Hindenburg and hoped to greet them, but they didn't look up.

It was nighttime when I found Cirilo Pintos, arms crossed, leaning back in a chair beneath a fluorescent light that cast a purple glow outside his house in Filadelfia's Indian neighborhood.

"What hurts us most as Indians is that the Mennonites don't want to recognize the contributions of our community," he said softly in Spanish.

Pintos seemed a little worried. A 39-year-old contractor, he depended on the Mennonites to keep him in business, and wondered whether speaking out would cost him.

Mennonites say they encountered a few hundred Indians, mostly Lenguas, when they arrived, though Indian-rights advocates argue the numbers were in the thousands. Both sides agree that as the Mennonite communities prospered—and as ranching pushed more Indians out of other parts of the Chaco—increasing numbers of Indians in search of work came to the settlements. Today about 14,000 of Paraguay's 100,000 Indians live alongside Mennonites.

The Mennonites are the Indians' teachers and employers: depending on the point of view, their benefactors or exploiters. Today this complex and interdependent relationship is changing as Indians like Pintos find their own voices.

Mennonites had taught Pintos to read and write, trained him in carpentry, hired him to work on their houses. Thanks to them, he has electricity and running water—amenities that many Paraguayans would envy.

Yet despite such opportunities, Pintos feels trapped by his second-class status. Without speaking German, his son cannot attend the local Mennonite high school. "A lot of Indian advocates think that we should return to our previous cultures," he said. "But for me this is absurd, I cannot go back."

MOST PARAGUAYANS have never seen the Chaco, yet it looms large in the national psyche. During the 1930s Paraguay beat Bolivia here, in a three-year territorial war that claimed the lives of more than 90,000 soldiers, 36,000 of them Paraguayan.

After winning the war, Paraguay's army never left the Chaco. The government stopped calling it a military zone in 1967, dividing the region into five departments, but civilian authority is nominal. Throughout the Chaco the military controls air traffic and border crossings and tends its numerous dirt roads.

"We have to maintain a presence here," said Maj. Vicente Adalberto Sandoval, as he drove me past a sea of dense green brush. "Because if not, Bolivia is going to want to come here once more."

The major and César Augusto, his four-year-old son, were my escorts through Mariscal Estigarribia, population 4,000, Paraguay's most military town. We drove by a U. S.-built airstrip, a post office, and a diesel-powered electric plant, all controlled by the army. The major showed me the town

Flaming bull horns blaze a trail of revelry through Yaguarón following a mass for the Virgen María Auxiliadora; in nearby Capiatá, brothers worship the Virgen del Rosario with music and prayer. For centuries a dominant part of Paraguayan life, the Roman Catholic Church now pushes for social change—from Indian rights to land reform.

A warm kiss and a cold beer signal the end of a spring day in Asunción. Prodded by South America's fastest growing population, Paraguay is slowly pulling out of the isolation of its past.

pharmacy, grocery store, and snack bar, owned by noncommissioned officers trying to supplement their meager military income.

Father and son dropped me off at the military hotel, where a sergeant showed me to my room, apologizing for the temporary lack of lights and water. First thing the next morning the major was back. "The general," he said, "is ready to see you."

The general was Emilio Osvaldo Balbuena, newly appointed head of the Third Army Corps and the Chaco's top military man. "There are no civilians willing to sacrifice themselves here," the general told me. "But I am delighted. This is a great challenge for me as a human being."

One tough question I didn't have to ask; the general brought it up himself, his mood somber. "Don't think that behind every general is a drug dealer," he said. "Does it seem strange to you that I'm 57 years old and I've never seen a drug?"

Long stretches of unguarded borders, coupled with the vast Chaco and its hundreds of remote landing strips, make Paraguay a natural transit point for Bolivian cocaine headed for Argentina and Brazil. For years accusations of complicity in the drug traffic have dogged the military's highest ranks.

General Balbuena wore his blue-green uniform with pride. A military man since 14, his eyes shone when he remembered Stroessner's overthrow. He had been in on the plot, he said. "I never agreed with Stroessner's clique," he told me.

The army's visible presence in the Chaco reflects Paraguay's wider picture: The military structure, so crucial to Stroessner's dictatorship, has yet to relinquish its power. "The process of democratization is irreversible," President Rodríguez has said. He has promised not to run again when his term expires in 1993 and has thrown his support behind a civilian successor. Yet for the moment the army continues to assume civilian roles, starting with President Rodríguez, still an active-duty general.

W HEN I RETURNED to Calle Palma in Asunción my last weekend in Paraguay, it was once again mobbed—this time by shoppers, not protesters, and the riot squad was nowhere to be found. It was Saturday morning, when cars are banned and the city's most elegant shopping street turns into a frenzied marketplace.

Piles of T-shirts, towels, and lingerie; trays of watches, music cassettes, and makeup; boxes of running shoes and exercise equipment lined block after block. *"Chipáaaas, chipás calienteees, chipáaaaas,"* chanted the women carrying pyramids of the warm

doughnut-shaped cakes of corn and cheese: "Chipás, hot chipás." To wash them down, vendors were pouring cold sugarcane juice.

Asuncenos who turn out for this Saturday scene along Calle Palma are said to be *Palmeando*—strolling Palma. It is an honored tradition, dating from the 1940s, when students would gather to play music and talk politics along the street's yellow tile sidewalks. Stroessner's permanent state of siege stifled the popular pastime. With the dictator now gone, Asuncenos pursue the sport with renewed enthusiasm.

That last Saturday in November, as Paraguayans prepared to elect the authors of a new constitution, a last-minute campaign fever gripped Calle Palma. Rival political parties blasted music, passed out pamphlets, and sold T-shirts in preparation for the election the following day.

As it turned out, the Colorados won 122 of 198 delegate slots; more of the same, said disheartened opponents. The 1989 coup did not bring democracy to Paraguay; it simply began the process.

That bright morning on Calle Palma, the future seemed full of possibilities. A sunny day, a crowded street, a departed dictator: deep in the belly of South America, an exhilarating sensation. ☐

Paraguay: Plotting a New Course

Still at attention, 2,100-year-old statues were conscripts in an amazing clay army now being unearthed at the tomb of Jing Di, fifth ruler of China's Han dynasty. Only two feet tall, the figures — their wooden arms and silk uniforms long decayed — were made to defend Jing Di in the afterlife.

ARTICLE AND
PHOTOGRAPHS BY
O. LOUIS
MAZZATENTA
SENIOR ASSISTANT EDITOR

A CHINESE EMPEROR'S
ARMY FOR

ETERNITY

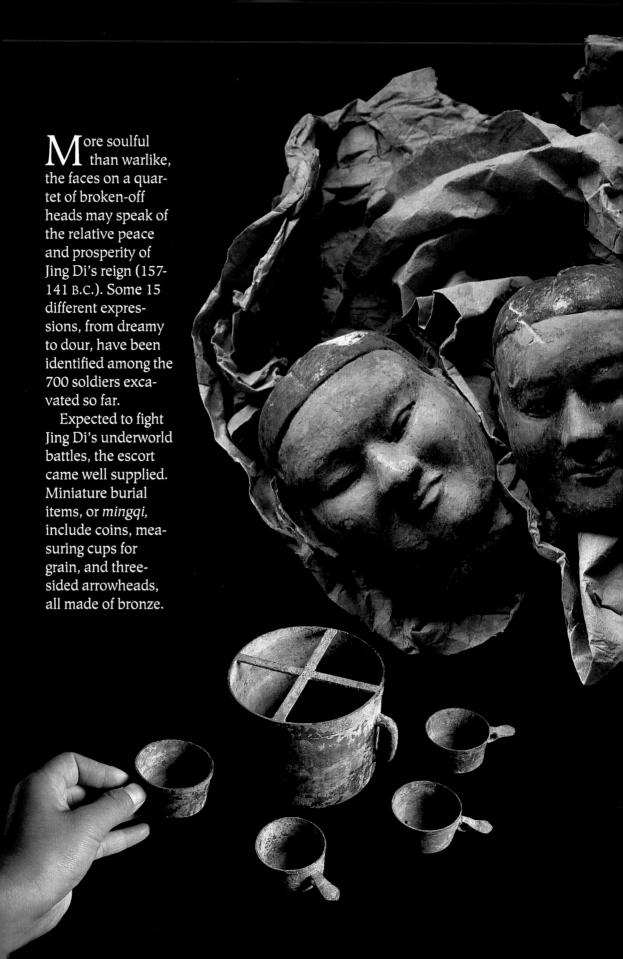

More soulful than warlike, the faces on a quartet of broken-off heads may speak of the relative peace and prosperity of Jing Di's reign (157-141 B.C.). Some 15 different expressions, from dreamy to dour, have been identified among the 700 soldiers excavated so far.

Expected to fight Jing Di's underworld battles, the escort came well supplied. Miniature burial items, or *mingqi*, include coins, measuring cups for grain, and three-sided arrowheads, all made of bronze.

"The smiles of Jing Di's soldiers linger in my mind's eye. They hint of secret delights."

NUDE AND ARMLESS, the buried terra-cotta army of Jing Di, fifth ruler of China's Han dynasty, is gradually emerging before my cameras. The workers have returned from the fields today to this dig near the ancient capital of Changan. They were interrupted last week by a higher priority—harvesting the corn. Now they are again scraping the dirt from a row of clay heads sprouting like cabbages from the floor of an earthen pit.

The dig, the first extensive excavation of a Han emperor's mausoleum, is one of China's most dramatic new archaeological discoveries. It lies in what my Chinese hosts call the sleeping town of emperors and their wives and concubines. More than 800 tombs have been located on this plain 12 miles from Xian (map, page 121). Some, such as the tomb of Jing Di himself (Di means emperor), rise like small mountains. None of the royal tombs have been opened yet. But now, as site director Wang Xueli of the Shaanxi Institute of Archaeology likes to say, "the sleeping town is wakening."

"MEN OF MUD," SO NAMED BY THE CHINESE PRESS, EMERGE IN ORDERLY RANKS IN PIT 20 (OPPOSITE). CAKED WITH DIRT, A HEAD IS GENTLY UNMASKED.

"In March 1990, workers were building a highway from Xian to the new airport," Wang explains. "The road passed Jing Di's tomb. The road builders noticed abnormalities in the soil and called us."

The archaeologists soon began digging into the fields beside the emperor's tomb and unearthed hundreds of elegantly crafted soldiers. Squads of these troops stood sentinel in parallel pits. Pieces of silk also found in the pits convince the scholars that the soldiers once wore fine garments, which, like their wooden arms, have disintegrated over the past 2,100 years.

This is the second imperial terra-cotta army found in China. The first, an honor guard of perhaps 10,000 life-size soldiers from the mausoleum of Qin Shi Huang Di, builder of the Great Wall, was discovered in 1974.*

At the Jing Di site, ground tests revealed a total of 24 pits; eight have been investigated so far, and they contain at least 700 figures. These are smaller—only two feet tall—than Qin Shi Huang Di's and differ in other ways.

"Qin Shi Huang Di's soldiers had their clothes sculptured and painted on them," says Wang Xueli. "Jing Di's army shows the beauty of nudity." There is beauty also in the faces of his buried soldiers, which show a wide range of human emotions.

"See that soldier with the prominent cheekbones," Wang says. "His round, bulging eyes make him seem like a fiery, forthright man. See that other one. He has a rich expression, such round jaws, and the natural complexion of a woman. I take him to be an honest and sincere fellow."

The faces of the two armies speak of different times and rulers. Qin Shi Huang Di, a charismatic despot who ruled from 221 to 210 B.C., united China for the first time. He also ordered the burning of books and had scholars and other opponents slaughtered.

Jing Di, who died about 70 years after Qin Shi Huang Di, is more obscure. His main achievement lay in suppressing the feudal rulers of kingdoms within the empire, thereby consolidating power in the central government. He paved the way for a long, glorious rule by his son, Wu Di. We know little about Jing Di's character, but he does seem to have had a temper. As a young man he was once playing a board game with a cousin from a

*See "China's Incredible Find," by Audrey Topping, NATIONAL GEOGRAPHIC, April 1978.

vassal kingdom, when a quarrel broke out. Jing Di ended it by crashing the wooden board over his cousin's skull, killing him.

In 1972 archaeologists uncovered the graveyard of an estimated 10,000 prisoners who died building Jing Di's tomb. Shackles were attached to the necks and legs of many skeletons. Some of the captives had been chopped in half; others must simply have been worked to death. Yet such atrocities probably reflect cruelties of the age more than Jing Di's personality.

Jing Di was descended from the Liu family, which rose to power after the death of Qin Shi Huang Di and founded the Han dynasty in 206 B.C. The Han concentrated on agriculture, diplomacy, and creating an infrastructure for their vast empire. Poetry was nurtured, paper was invented, and woven silk became a major export. The Han fortified the famous Silk Road against marauding nomads of Central Asia, so it could funnel riches between China and cities as far west as Rome.

The Han dynasty was a golden age. Life in the imperial court was lavish, and it swirled with intrigue as the emperor's wives and their families vied for influence.

"Whenever Lady Li meets any of the ladies of the inner palace who are more honored and favored than herself," one sniping princess is reported to have confided, "she has her attendants utter curses and magic spells and spit behind their backs. She is practicing sorcery in an attempt to win your [the emperor's] affections!"

JING DI'S NETWORK of pits will never give us such colorful insights into life at court, but the well-stocked vaults do promise to confirm many details about ancient Chinese views of death.

Since reading of the discovery, I had been eager to photograph the emperor's soldiers. Ancient burials fascinate me: For past stories I spent weeks in the tombs of Egyptians and Etruscans, and now I am focusing my camera on ground another culture believed was alive with spirits. I feel in all these sites a presence that must be respected.

A heap of bones in pit 20 reveals ways of life

A Chinese Emperor's Army for Eternity

as well as of death. The bones are those of a tomb robber, and they now lie next to a hole he appears to have dug (page 128).

"Unlucky man," says deputy site director Wang Bao Ping, picking up a brick near the bones. "This is probably what killed him. It looks like his partner didn't want to share the loot. . . . Or maybe it was just an accident."

Another accident in a desecrated tomb was recorded by a Han historian. A brigade of robbers entered the tomb of Empress Lü, wife of the first Han emperor, 200 years after her death in 180 B.C. and violated her body. A fire erupted, perhaps when incoming oxygen mixed with tomb gases, and many of them died.

In addition to the grave robber's bones, pit 20 contains numerous red lacquered boxes bound with metal belts. Time has destroyed some of the belts. Intruders may have broken others. Excavators have not yet opened the boxes, which Wang Xueli believes are filled with weapons; the pit probably served as a model armory.

Each pit seems to have a different theme, promising glimpses of a specific aspect of Han life. In pit 17, for instance, 70 terra-cotta soldiers were found marching behind two carriages, each drawn by three wooden horses, now largely decayed. Workers also dug up bronze horse bits and carriage axles as well as miniature arrowheads and a crossbow trigger. Most interesting, though, part of the pit was filled ten feet high with grain. This must have been a granary for the army.

Pit 21 contains sculptured animals—two oxen, four dogs, four sheep, and two pigs. A clay soldier lies beside two iron cooking pots. Close by are two large ceramic soup bowls and many smaller ones, also for food. "It looks like an army chow line," one expert says.

JING DI'S PITS illustrate the role of the emperor in Han times. Considered divine, he was believed to intercede with heaven for his people, whose prosperity depended on him. He was, moreover, a master of mystification, living in splendid isolation. "He was too sacred to name," says Han expert Jeffrey Riegel of the University of California at Berkeley. The emperor was therefore often addressed by the words meaning "foot of the stairs"—the highest a person could look in his presence.

So when Foot of the Stairs died, the burial was an immense exaggeration of the ordinary mortal's funeral customs—but less extreme than those of earlier rulers who had scores of their servants, artists, and concubines buried alive with them.

Tomb excavations during the past 40 years are evidence of the Han belief that the afterlife was a prolongation of this life. Thus Jing Di's mausoleum, as his afterworld headquarters, would have mirrored the magnificence of his residence on earth. The tombs of the rich were lavishly provisioned; goods brought along—everything from finely woven silks and musical instruments to food and drink—indicated a life well lived. Whereas a common man might be buried with a miniature clay granary, the emperor got a full-size granary as well as his own army.

The army might be needed after death. Jing Di once accused a loyal general of buying too many weapons for his own tomb. The man was charged with the intent to lead a rebellion against the emperor in the afterlife. Imprisoned and humiliated, the proud officer starved himself to death.

LONG AFTER I RETURN from China, the smiles of Jing Di's soldiers linger in my mind's eye. They hint of secret delights. I ask a Han scholar at Harvard University, Wu Hung, what that dreamy transcendent expression represents. He speculates that the smiles reflect a new way of thinking about the afterlife: In the quest for immortality the dark underworld becomes a realm of eternal happiness.

Jing Di was apparently taken with the philosophy of Taoism, which was then so popular. In contrast to Confucianism, with its emphasis on discipline, public service, ceremony, and morality, Taoism looked inward, seeking harmony with nature. It discouraged conventional social customs and favored tolerance, simplicity, and spontaneity—qualities that Jing Di's soldiers seem to convey.

"The artists couldn't create whatever they wanted," Wu says. "This was funerary art commissioned by the emperor, to be buried in the dark where only he would see it."

Do the soldiers' expressions of apparent contentment indicate Jing Di's view of death? Wu Hung says it is too early to answer this question. Perhaps as the excavations continue, we will come closer to understanding the secret of those smiles.

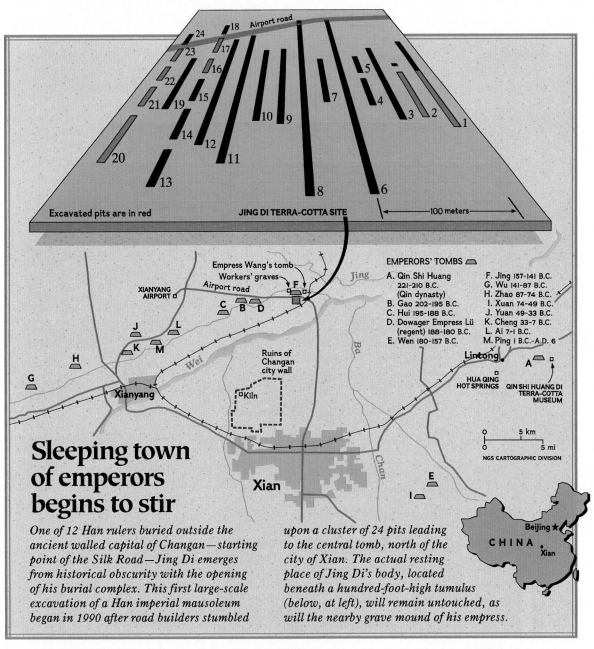

Airport road

24 18
23 17
16
22
21 19 15
14
20 12
11
13

10 9

7

5
4
3 2 1

8 6

Excavated pits are in red

JING DI TERRA-COTTA SITE

|← 100 meters →|

Empress Wang's tomb
Workers' graves
Airport road

Jing

XIANYANG
AIRPORT

F

C
B D

EMPERORS' TOMBS

A. Qin Shi Huang
   221-210 B.C.
   (Qin dynasty)
B. Gao 202-195 B.C.
C. Hui 195-188 B.C.
D. Dowager Empress Lü
   (regent) 188-180 B.C.
E. Wen 180-157 B.C.

F. Jing 157-141 B.C.
G. Wu 141-87 B.C.
H. Zhao 87-74 B.C.
I. Xuan 74-49 B.C.
J. Yuan 49-33 B.C.
K. Cheng 33-7 B.C.
L. Ai 7-1 B.C.
M. Ping 1 B.C.-A.D. 6

J
K
M
L

Ba

Wei

H

G

Xianyang

Ruins of
Changan
city wall

Kiln

Lintong

HUA QING
HOT SPRINGS

A

QIN SHI HUANG DI
TERRA-COTTA
MUSEUM

Chan

0   5 km
0   5 mi
NGS CARTOGRAPHIC DIVISION

Sleeping town of emperors begins to stir

One of 12 Han rulers buried outside the ancient walled capital of Changan—starting point of the Silk Road—Jing Di emerges from historical obscurity with the opening of his burial complex. This first large-scale excavation of a Han imperial mausoleum began in 1990 after road builders stumbled upon a cluster of 24 pits leading to the central tomb, north of the city of Xian. The actual resting place of Jing Di's body, located beneath a hundred-foot-high tumulus (below, at left), will remain untouched, as will the nearby grave mound of his empress.

Xian

Beijing ★
CHINA
Xian

T oppled like duckpins when the roof of an underground vault caved in long ago, ranks of broken soldiers in pit 17 await removal to a restoration lab. Besides the iron swords still slung from their hips, the statues each carried a wooden shield and a spearlike halberd, few of which have survived intact.

In earlier dynasties real soldiers—as well as servants, artisans, and concubines—were buried alive in an emperor's tomb. Human sacrifice was disappearing by the time Qin Shi Huang Di, who built the Great Wall, died in 210 B.C. At the site of his mausoleum, archaeologists in 1974 found an army of statues, all life-size.

Less than 70 years after Qin Shi Huang Di, Jing Di moved even further toward the purely symbolic by commissioning burial soldiers that stood only one-third life-size.

Because no archers, cavalry forces, or armored infantrymen have yet been found, excavators believe these first pits hold rearguard supply troops. Soldiers were uncovered with tools, stocks of grain, ceramic pigs, sheep, and a pair of shattered, two-foot-long oxen, the largest ever found in a Han tomb (right). Chief archaeologist Wang Xueli expects that more elaborately armed frontline soldiers, perhaps in the thousands, will be discovered in other pits.

In pit 17 the troops appear to be guarding a large granary. Excavators sifting through dirt (top) have found enough wheat, corn, and millet—well preserved after two millennia—to fill a stack of baskets.

Then, as now, growing food to feed the masses was a national duty. Within a day of the photographer's visit to pit 17, the trench was filled in, and farmers were sowing wheat on the surface.

WANG BAO PING (LEFT)

To populate the emperor's tomb, a cast of thousands was summoned from the workshops and kilns of the imperial court. A painting based on kilns recently excavated outside Xian depicts how Han laborers mass-produced the doll-like statues (opposite).

The figures emerged in pieces from molds, four for each body. One mold, for the back of the upper body, is shown cradling a statue (right). Facial features incised on the molds were so expressive that some experts believe artisans used fellow workers as models.

Moist clay was pressed into the molds with a tamp, such as the one that left behind the impression of a frog, a good-luck symbol (right). The body molds were sealed together with clay and inserted upside down into a wood-fired kiln, about 300 to a chamber, where they baked for four days.

The terra-cotta, or fired-clay, statues were then taken to

workshops to be painted, fitted with arms, dressed in silk, and equipped with weapons.

Over the centuries the figures were damaged as wooden ceilings and pillars collapsed on them. At a converted farmhouse, restorers (below) mend cracked bodies. The decision has not yet been made whether to preserve the statues on site or in a new museum.

PAINTING BY BURT SILVERMAN

"Treat death as life," counsels an old Chinese saying—one that inspired Jing Di, like all the early, war-plagued emperors, to make his tomb battle ready. Laborers stocked the chambers (left) with legions of figurines whose wooden arms rotated at the shoulder, the better to wield weapons in afterlife battles. An inspector checks the sturdiness of one outfitted warrior.

Female figures, possibly courtesans or servants, were also installed. The few discovered thus far show traces of silk clothing.

Little is left of the soldiers' uniforms. A rare fragment of cloth from a headband, having slipped down over a statue's ears, is preserved under a sealed bell jar (top).

Dirt-encrusted leggings, painted with lacquer, show up on a restored statue (right). Bands of white mark where the fragile limb sections were glued back together.

Jing Di's longevity grave, begun soon after he succeeded his father, Wen Di, took at least ten years to construct, draining the imperial treasury. The human cost was enormous as well. A graveyard discovered nearby held the remains of an estimated 10,000 people, many of them prisoner-laborers who were likely worked to death building their ruler's tomb.

Fallen figures, clay and human, litter the floors of opened pits. A portion of the emperor's miniature army lies in pieces in what may have been the armory (opposite). The yet unopened wooden boxes, preserved by their original coat of red lacquer, are believed to contain a cache of weapons.

Elsewhere, on an intact plank floor, a clay soldier lies beside iron and ceramic cooking bowls (above), possibly signs of a mess hall to feed the army.

For all its weaponry, the terra-cotta army was defenseless against tomb robbers. One pit when dug up was found to have been nearly emptied by thieves; two others showed signs of looting.

The getaway went awry for one trespasser long ago. At the bottom of a tunnel burrowed into pit 20—site of Jing Di's armory—excavators recovered a skeleton with its skull bashed in (right); a brick lay nearby. Was the death an accident, or was the victim done in by a greedy partner?

Officials at the tomb reckon the incident took place in the first century A.D., during a widespread peasant uprising. At the time, many imperial tombs were looted.

That grave robbing continues was signaled by the recent appearance in the New York art market of several high-priced terra-cotta figures similar in style to Jing Di's. One of them is thought to have come from a later Han emperor's tomb and was appraised at between $7,000 and $9,000.

Fertile ground for history and a field of crops, the land around Jing Di's burial mound nourishes farmer Liu Xing Rang, out hoeing with his bashful grandson. The past often resurfaces, in the form of ancient roof tiles, when Liu turns the soil. Some 40 noble families built tombs near Jing Di's mausoleum. A town of 15,000 people was also built to ensure that offerings would be made to the late emperor. Even today families seeking good fortune bury their dead near the imposing grave.

Who was the man Jing Di? Excavations so far reveal little. The record states dryly that Jing Di furthered the unification of China, encouraged agriculture, and started a civil service.

"He was neither saint nor Satan," says University of Pittsburgh scholar Hsu Cho-yun. "He was a ruthless leader who provided order and security. A despot, yes, but remember, he had to be imperial." □

WILDLIFE AS CANON SEES IT

CRESTED HONEYCREEPER RANGE

Oahu
Molokai
Lanai
Kahoolawe
Maui
HAWAII
USA
Hawaii
Pacific Ocean

Crested Honeycreeper

Genus: *Palmeria*

Species: *dolei*

Adult size: Length, 18 cm

Adult weight: Approx. 32 g

Habitat: Ohia forests on the island of Maui, USA

Surviving number: Estimated at 2,000

Photographed by Jack Jeffrey

Known also by its Hawaiian name, "akohekohe," the crested honeycreeper survives only in a narrow belt of rainforest on the upper slopes of Haleakala volcano on Maui. Researchers discovered the first known nests of the crested honeycreeper only recently. With the discovery, biologists can now better study the ecology of this rare bird, offering greater hope for its survival. To save endangered species, it is essential to protect their habitats and understand the vital role of each species within the earth's ecosystems. Photography, both as a scientific research tool and as a means of communication, can help promote a greater awareness and understanding of the crested honeycreeper and our entire wildlife heritage.

EOS 1
The New Classic

NATURE

Watch "NATURE" on PBS, Sunday 8:00 p.m.
This program is funded, in part, by Canon U.S.A., Inc.

Canon

On Television

The Men Behind the Monuments

A mud-brick grave on the Giza plateau outside Cairo yielded its secret—the 4,500-year-old skeleton of a construction worker (right)—piece by piece. At the time, National Geographic producer Steve Burns was preoccupied with his camera, balancing the harsh Egyptian sunlight with the blackness of the grave. But as diggers tilted the skull, and tears of sand poured from its eyes, Burns forgot about the technicalities. "I suddenly felt connected with this individual from the distant past," he says.

His film, "Who Built the Pyramids?" featured on EXPLORER's 1992-93 season premiere, investigates what may be the largest construction site of the ancient world. Here on the banks of the Nile an estimated 30,000 people labored to raise the mightiest of all monuments, the Great Pyramids.

These tombs of kings have fascinated generations, but now the discovery of a vast workers cemetery on the site "tells us about the lives of common men," says Zahi Hawass, director general of the Pyramids for the Egyptian Antiquities

TIM STEINBERG

Organization. More than 250 graves and 14 tombs have been uncovered so far. The obvious care that went into them suggests that the Pyramid builders were not slaves but free men, perhaps conscripted farmers.

About 300 yards from the cemetery Mark Lehner of the University of Chicago unearthed a huge bakery, where every day bread for thousands of people was baked in bell-shaped clay pots. "Bringing together this large group of people," Lehner says, "marked a distinct

threshold in our worldwide heritage—the rise of urbanism. This was the equivalent of downtown Cairo."

Who Built the Pyramids? EXPLORER Season Premiere, Aug. 30, TBS Super-Station, 9 p.m. ET.

Educational Films: 20 Years in the Classroom

Back in 1972 the National Geographic Society launched its Educational Films Division, headed by Sidney Platt. Since then the division, with a staff of nine, has set the standard for classroom films, winning virtually every major award in the industry. "All aspects of our work—the ideas, the scripts, the editing—are designed to aid learning," says Platt, who still charts the course.

Ed Films produces 15 to 20 new films each year—more than 300 titles so far—to let viewers explore the farthest reaches of the globe (left) and the microscopic world within a cell. The films reach their audience by combining the entertainment of TV or the movies with the information of a textbook.

"We challenge students by using technology that we know will hold their attention," says associate director Donald Cooper. "After all, many of our staff have kids who watch these films in school."

ANNE B. KEISER

The 1992 Plymouth Acclaim is America's best-equipped six-passenger car for under $12,700. Equipped with a standard driver's air bag, it costs $2,900 less than Accord.* Yet it has more interior space and rear passenger room. Acclaim also offers greater available power than Accord. Plus our Owner's Choice Protection Plan: a 7 year/70,000 mile powertrain warranty, *or* a 3 year/36,000 mile bumper to bumper warranty.† No other car maker in the world offers you this level of flexibility in choosing warranty protection. Visit your Chrysler-Plymouth dealer today. Or call 1-800-PLYMOUTH for purchasing or Gold Key Plus/leasing information.

Advantage: Plymouth
CHRYSLER *Plymouth* A DIVISION OF CHRYSLER CORPORATION

HANDLES WELL IN TIGHT FINANCIAL SITUATIONS.

1992 Plymouth Acclaim

*Base MSRP $11,470. Price with 22D option package and six-passenger seating $12,682. Title, tax and destination fee extra. Standard equipment levels vary. †See limited warranties at dealer. Restrictions apply. 3/36 excludes normal maintenance, adjustments & wear items. **Buckle up for safety!** © Plymouth/Chrysler Corp., 1992. 36USC380.

OFFICIAL SPONSOR OF THE
1992 U.S. OLYMPIC TEAM

Earth Almanac

GUNTER ZIESLER, PETER ARNOLD, INC.

Eco-Businesses Grow — and the Earth Profits

Dan Bernard (below) remembers all too well what the Androscoggin River looked like when he was growing up in Lewiston, Maine. "It was just disgusting—covered with yellow scum from factories and mills."

Spurred by such unpleasant memories, Dan now runs a mail-order operation out of Lewiston, one of more than 200 small U. S. businesses specializing in environmentally friendly products. He offers a "better" mousetrap—one with a "freedom door," allowing the customer to release the unwelcome rodent in an appropriate habitat. In addition to this planet mug, there

M. PHILIP KAHL, DRK PHOTO

is a foam look-alike cup made of porcelain bearing the message "Styrofoam is Forever."

Other items:
- Bird feeders, backyard benches, and yo-yos made of recycled plastic.
- A ballpoint pen with a recycled-paper barrel.
- A rechargeable, solar-powered AM/FM transistor radio.
- A portable ozone generator to eliminate powerful odors and kill bacteria indoors.

Dan is also a dealer for a solar-electric sports car called the Destiny 2000, built by Solar Electric Engineering, Inc., and featured in the recent motion picture *Naked Gun 2½*.

SHAWN G. HENRY, SABA

Shielded by Volcanoes, Flamingos Still Need Help

High in the Andes where howling winds and bitter cold create seemingly lifeless landscapes, a dreamlike vision appears. Beneath snowcapped volcanoes, Andean flamingos strain algae and roundworms from shallow salt pans. About 150,000 flamingos of three species—Andean, James's, and Chilean—survive in lakes within a 120,000-square-mile slice of Peru, Bolivia, Chile, and Argentina.

Yet even amid such isolation, local people harvest flamingo eggs to sell as food. Females lay a single egg, and the nesting pair raises the lone chick (above left). To protect one flock from eggers, the Chilean Forestry Department has provided rangers since 1985. The project is supported by Wildlife Conservation International, part of the New York Zoological Society. But WCI general director William Conway warns, "Egging still goes on in Bolivia."

He also reports a mystery: Chile's 75,000 flamingos have declined to 7,000 in four years. "What has happened? Where are they?" he wonders. "We thought they moved to Argentina—they didn't. Now we think they're in Bolivia."

Earth Almanac

Walrus Headhunter Arrests Echo in Alaska

Climaxing a three-year undercover probe, last February law-enforcement personnel swept over Alaska's west coast in Operation Whiteout. Some 80 Alaska natives and nonnatives are expected to be charged with offenses related to hunting walruses for their tusks. Much ivory allegedly was exchanged for drugs, such as marijuana and cocaine (far right).

Only coastal natives may hunt the protected walrus, and only if the animal is used for food, traditional carvings, clothing, and skin boats. Though native communities aided the operation, many still fear a public backlash from the mass arrests. Says Bruce Batten of the U. S. Fish and Wildlife Service in Anchorage, "We don't think that this is typical of native walrus hunting."

JOHNNY JOHNSON, ALLSTOCK

BRUCE BATTEN, U. S. FISH AND WILDLIFE SERVICE

Nudibranchs Recycle Weapons of Their Prey

Why do jellyfish stings hurt so much? A fish-eye view of the pain-inducing mechanism would terrify bathers. Jellyfish, corals, sea fans, anemones, and hydroids are armed with stinging cells, murderously miraculous in design. Each cell contains a nematocyst with a long, coiled thread inside

MIKE NEUMANN, PHOTO RESEARCHERS

Changing the Danube's Blues to a Healthier Green

Johann Strauss would be appalled. The river that inspired "The Blue Danube" waltz has become constricted by dams and fouled by pollution from its Black Forest source to its Black Sea mouth. The 1,770-mile-long Danube serves as a sewer for more than 400 million people living in a dozen nations. The Main-Danube Canal (map, pages 10-11) will likely add to heavy traffic, as at the Romanian port of Galați (below). But

environmental sentiment is growing. Since 1986, protests have halted two proposed dams, including a massive Czechoslovak-Hungarian scheme.

Now the World Wide Fund for Nature and other groups want to change Strauss's tune with the Green Danube Project. Riverside national parks would be created in Germany, Czechoslovakia, Austria, Hungary, Yugoslavia, and Romania, with emphasis on the 2,000 square miles of wetlands in the Danube Delta. A separate plan would pressure several of the nations to clean up their Danube waters.

that can explode like a tiny harpoon into prey or enemy. There are about 20 types of nematocysts. Some entangle, some stick like glue, and some inject a toxin that both immobilizes and digests.

But some creatures can protect themselves, and the past masters are certain sea slugs, or nudibranchs (above). These mollusks feed on organisms that bear stinging cells, coating them with mucus so the weapons are not triggered as they pass through the sea slugs' bodies. Amazingly the nematocysts wind up inside the frilly fronds on the backs of the sea slugs, which then become armed and dangerous.

—John L. Eliot

ADAM WOOLFITT, SUSAN GRIGGS AGENCY

We Can't Tell You What He'll Be Listening To A Year From Now.

But With Eveready® Rechargeables, He Could Be Listening To It On The Same Set Of Batteries.

Chances are, techno-pop will replace rap before you have to replace Eveready® Rechargeables. Even though rechargeables don't last as long per use as alkaline batteries, they're a great value in the long run. In fact, Eveready® Rechargeables can be recharged and used over and over again.*

To recharge, just pop your AAA, AA, C, D or 9V Eveready® Rechargeable batteries in our 3- or 5-hour chargers and soon you'll be set to go. Keep a spare pair in the charger and you'll always be prepared.

So look for Eveready® Rechargeables. You'll save money, not to mention a few trips to the store. And that should be music to your ears.

*In laboratory tests, Eveready® Rechargeables were recharged 500 times.

EVEREADY®
RECHARGEABLES

On Assignment

Free-lancer ED KASHI tries to capture the most dramatic moment in any encounter. Photographing embattled Kurds from Damascus to Düsseldorf, his first assignment for the GEOGRAPHIC, offered such opportunities—and some risk. For weeks Ed traveled in northern Iraq with these well-armed *peshmerga* guerrillas guarding against Saddam Hussein's forces.

The real picture was not always where he expected. Ed accompanied a Kurdish human-rights lawyer for several days on risky travels in southeastern Turkey. At a federal "terrorist court" in Diyarbakır, Ed made frame after frame of the lawyer defending his client, but the angle was wrong. Then he turned around and snapped a single frame of the defendant (pages 50-51). With that, the judge made him sit down and put his camera away.

Taking chances is nothing new to the San Francisco-based photojournalist. Ed spent more than two years in strife-torn Northern Ireland, which yielded photo exhibits along with the publication *No Surrender: The Protestants.* He is now back in the Middle East looking at its water problems for a future GEOGRAPHIC.

To spend time with an army near Xian in China—one with soldiers

ED KASHI

two feet tall and 2,100 years old— LOU MAZZATENTA literally went underground last year. Working in pits 20 feet deep, Lou (below, with remains of ceramic oxen) became the first Western journalist to

photograph the miniatures in the tomb of the Han ruler Jing Di.

The excavators made him feel welcome, and the terra-cotta statues themselves created a social air. "As I photographed the soldiers coming out of the ground, they seemed like real people," he marvels. "Their human expressions made them look as if they were thinking, 'Hey, what took you so long to find us?' "

The Jing Di excavation marks Lou's fifth archaeological story in his 29-year GEOGRAPHIC career. A senior assistant editor in charge of magazine scheduling, he has photographed the Appian Way, Herculaneum, Etruscan civilization, and Egypt's Ramses the Great.

"What fascinates me about archaeology," he says, "is that it is ancient history made new. Things are revealed for the first time, and you feel your work is more important for that." For his next story Lou will go even deeper into the past, photographing invertebrate fossils 550 million years old.

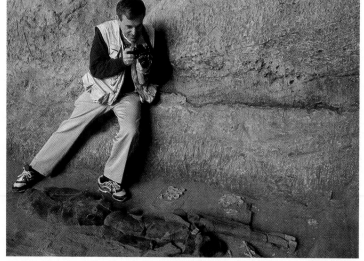

ZHOU JIANSHEN

NATIONAL GEOGRAPHIC (ISSN 0027-9358) IS PUBLISHED MONTHLY BY THE NATIONAL GEOGRAPHIC SOCIETY, 17TH AND M STS. N.W., WASHINGTON, D. C. 20036. $21.00 A YEAR, $2.65 A COPY. SECOND-CLASS POSTAGE PAID AT WASHINGTON, D. C., AND ELSEWHERE. POSTMASTER: SEND ADDRESS CHANGES TO NATIONAL GEOGRAPHIC, P.O. BOX 2174, WASHINGTON, D. C. 20013.

Why wash your dishes before you wash your dishes?

Introducing the new Maytag Jetclean™ dishwasher.

Every day millions of Americans do something strange: they wash their dishes and then put them in the dishwasher.

But this is the new Maytag Jetclean dishwasher. And it's going to change all that. With 43 powerful jets that scrub from the top, bottom and sides, a filter and a disposer, it's designed to clean dishes without pre-rinsing. And

© 1992 Maytag Co.

with our new six-tier racking system, everything from small glasses to large cookie sheets is exposed to all that cleaning power.

While all that scrubbing is going on inside, you'll never know it on the outside. Fact is, you won't find a major brand that's quieter than our Dependably Quiet™ Plus models.

So forget your scrub brushes, sponges and scouring pads. And get yourself a new Maytag Jetclean dishwasher. Once you do, you'll wonder why you ever washed your dishes any other way.

MAYTAG
® THE DEPENDABILITY PEOPLE

COROLLA

Corolla. Over 15 million happy memories, and still counting.

Your parents' car. Your first car. The car you learned to drive in. Millions of people have fond memories of a Toyota Corolla.

And though we've made lots of changes to the Corolla over the years, the soul of the car has always stayed the same. It's still known as reliable. Practical. And economical.*

Which may be why, over the last 25 years, we've made more than just 15 million† Corollas.

We've also built lots of lasting relationships.

"I love what you do for me."

TOYOTA